PRAISE FOR REVELATION AND RESPONSE

"*Revelation and Response* is a timely prescription for the health of the modern music leader. Parkison helps us think biblically, theologically, and practically about the scope of Christian worship; and he skillfully applies these truths to our practice of corporate worship."

–**Matt Boswell**, Hymnwriter and Pastor at *The Trails Church*

"Christians today must battle confusion on many fronts. We may be no more confused than in our understanding of corporate worship. In *Revelation and Response*, a gifted young writer seeks to build out a proper understanding of the most valuable endeavor humanity can undertake: to worship the living God. Sam Parkison's theological meditation on corporate worship is at once moving and practical, inspiring and critical. It will fire up the next generation to sing, pray, and offer our lives as a living sacrifice in response to the works of our awesome God."

–**Dr. Owen Strachan**, Associate Professor of Christian Theology, Midwestern Seminary; author, *Risky Gospel*

"Local church gatherings across the evangelical spectrum are often marked by shallow sermons, pithy prayers, and mushy music. But Samuel G. Parkison offers us a better way, one marked by a deep theology of corporate worship that lifts our gaze to the majesty of the living God. Sam's wisdom and pastoral heart have encouraged me since the day I met him, and this book is a microcosm of why more people should listen to him."

–**Brandon D. Smith**, Editorial Director for the Center for Baptist Renewal and author of *Rooted: Theology for Growing Christians*

"If you read one book on worship, this is the book you should read. In my ministry of working with dying and declining churches across North America, I encounter churches who are starving for authentic Christ-centered worship. In this book Samuel G. Parkison provides a comprehensive, biblical approach to true corporate worship. There is no doubt that authentic church revitalization cannot happen without biblical, authentic, corporate worship. I wholeheartedly commend this book to every pastor and every church, but specifically for those churches that are struggling with the decline."

–**Mark Clifton**, Senior Director Church Replanting for the North American Mission Board of The Southern Baptist Convention, and author of *Reclaiming Glory: Revitalizing Dying Churches*

"So many books on worship fall into one of two opposite dilemmas—they are either too academically dry or too stylistically contemporary, both of which have the tendency of stifling the awe intrinsic to Christian worship. This is why I'm thankful for Samuel G. Parkison's *Revelation and Response*, which is theologically weighty but artful and immediately practical without giving itself a sell-by date. Sam's heart for pastoring God's people into a worship that is bigger than Sunday morning music can only help your Sunday morning music get bigger."

–**Jared C. Wilson**, Director of Content Strategy for Midwestern Baptist Theological Seminary, managing editor of For The Church, and author of more than ten books, including *Gospel Wakefulness*, *The Pastor's Justification*, and *The Prodigal Church*

REVELATION & RESPONSE

THE WHY AND HOW OF LEADING CORPORATE WORSHIP THROUGH SONG

Samuel G. Parkison

Revelation and Response: The Why and How of
Leading Corporate Worship through Song

ISBN 978-1-948022-09-5

Rainer Publishing
www.RainerPublishing.com
Spring Hill, TN

Printed in the United States of America

To the saints at Emmaus Church, Kansas City.
Pastoring you is among the greatest honors of my life.

CONTENTS

INTRODUCTION

Yes, this is *another* book about worship. The seeming redundancy is not lost on me; the Christian book market has no shortage of worship-ministry books, so why *this one*? The simple answer is: time doesn't stand still. If two thousand years of church history has taught us anything, it is that the innovators are often the heretics; faithful stewardship with the "faith once for all delivered to the saints" simply looks like repeating the same timeless truths in a new day. Nothing you find in this book will be novel; it's all been said before by dead saints who said it to their generations, and someday when you and I are dead, men and women will (Lord willing) follow suit. But you and I are not living a yesterday or tomorrow—today is our day.

My aim in writing this book is to provide something useful for the church today. What you hold in your hands is a music leader's survival guide. Like any good survival guide, it is not exhaustive in any of the areas it explores, but it does include the bare essentials of what you need. I believe every person up front leading the congregation in music should have some sort of basic, working knowledge of everything covered in this book. So feel free to mine it for its usefulness to your own ministerial context. I want this book to be profitable; it was intended to be read in sequential order, but it would not offend me if you gutted it for helpful information.

If this book is a building project, chapter 1 is demolition. So much of modern evangelicalism's notion of "worship" is structurally unsound, so the first chapter is basically deconstructive. Chapter 2 lays the theological foundation for the rest of the book, which covers the crucial distinction between worship and worship *through song*. Chapters 3 and 4 address daily worship. The fifth chapter identifies the tension every Christian ought to feel on account of worship in a fallen world—the reality of the Christian's status as a resident alien, a citizen of the already/not-yet kingdom of Jesus. Chapters 6 and 7 are the most directly applicable chapters to the activity of congregational worship through song; they include a dissection of the "music leader" platform and the congregational worship service itself. Chapter 8 is a shameless soap box upon which I stand to do nothing more than revel in the gospel.

Also, one thing you may recognize when reading this book is the suspiciously rare usage of the title "worship leader." You won't see me readily use the title for the people up front with the instruments. Instead, I'll say, "music leader," or "musical-worship leader," or "those who lead worship through song." This is owing to the fact that, yes, I am *one of those* curmudgeons. I do believe that in the broader evangelical world the *title* of "worship leader" is more harmful than helpful, since it implies that worship happens when the "worship leader" is *leading*. In other words, the title insinuates that no activity outside of that which the "worship leader" engages in should be understood as worship. But this is misleading. The music people don't have a monopoly on the word "worship." Don't worry, I'm not here to make you feel bad about using the title "worship leader." That's not the purpose of this book. In fact, you won't see me call attention to my title preferences for the rest of this book, because I'm not really concerned with that. Instead, by quietly swapping the popular title with my clunky alternatives, I'm trying to shift the needle on how we understand the word "worship" (namely, that it cannot be reduced to *song*). Don't mind me as I plant this idea in your brain, all *inception-like*. Don't even think about what I'm doing. Just keep reading.

One more word needs to be said about the intended audience. I'm directly speaking to music leaders—everyone from the teenager who, after mastering his fourth chord on the guitar, was just pushed on stage in the youth room, to the seasoned pastor who leads his congregation in worship through song every week. I also have an eye toward other pastors. Not every music leader is also a pastor, but every pastor should be concerned with the songs his congregation sings. So, non-music-leading pastors, even though I'm not primarily addressing you in this book, I will from time to time, so please continue to listen in on the discussion. Lastly, most of the book deals with worship not in the narrow musical sense but in the broad biblical sense, which makes it applicable to every Christian. So if you are a Christian who lacks musical inclination, but you still want to be a faithful worshiper of Jesus, I trust and pray much of this book will remain helpful and edifying for you.

CHAPTER 1

WHAT CORPORATE WORSHIP SHOULD NOT BE

The term "corporate worship" conjures up a lot of different images. Some of those images are appropriate and should be there, but many ideas of corporate worship have arisen from years of weird developments in an evangellyfishy subculture. We need to paint a picture of biblical corporate worship for the aspirations of the leaders, and in order for this to happen, we need to work with a blank canvas. So think of this first chapter as a bucket of primer. I hope you'll forgive me, reader, if some of your cherished ideas are painted over; hopefully the finished product will be beautiful enough to compensate for any temporary offenses!

A SNAPSHOT OF HIP EVANGELICALISM

What's the ideal worship experience? What should we see and not see? What makes a worship experience authentic? Much of evangelicalism may answer that question with this kind of description: "The ideal worship service is one where God really shows up and moves! The music is expressive and free. The lights are dimmed. Everyone has their eyes closed, and they're unconcerned with the people around them. It's just time for you and God." You get the idea. There is a distinct mood—an ambiance. What comes to mind is that fluttering of the heart and the heightened awareness of the senses. It's not too heady, because it's "real."

We're all familiar with these kinds of gatherings, right? That sort of in-between stage of being not quite awake and not quite asleep. Essentially, what we want is a private time with Jesus, and we expect that time to produce a particular feeling. Hear me say this: *feelings are not wrong.* I'm not here to advocate for orthodusty stoicism. In fact, feelings *must* be engaged for worship of the living God to be authentic and honoring to him. But here's the point: although every participant in such a gathering *is* worshiping, many of them may not be worshiping the Triune God of the Bible.

SINGING IN SOCAL

Maybe I should share a little bit about my own experience with this kind of mushy emotionalism. I grew up in a non-denominational church movement that started in Southern California. Depending on which one of these churches you walk into, you might find a lot of charismatic activity going on, or you might think that you just stumbled into the average evangelical church. Think somewhere between Pentecostals and Southern Baptists—Bapticostals, if you will. The particular church that I grew up in was pretty balanced; occasionally you'd get some exciting moments, but for the most part people seemed content to sit quietly without making a ruckus.

Eventually I found myself in Southern California, where I spent a year of my undergraduate career as a student at this church movement's flagship Bible college. My experience there was mostly great. I made some life-long friendships, experienced significant community, went through a bit of a theological pilgrimage, and it was there I initially felt called into pastoral ministry. I also developed a distinct "dude-ness" in my dialect, but that wore off over time, among other things. One such "other thing" was my perspective on worship.

You can probably guess what our "spontaneous" worship gatherings looked like. My friends were the quintessential beach-bum Christians; the "let's-just-surf-and-chill-out-with-Jesus-brah" kind of fellows, which means there was a kind of Christian zen to our activity. This isn't difficult to imagine when you take our context into account; we were located in Murrieta, California, where the palm trees flourish and the sun is always shining. Frankly, it was easy to mellow out.

In front of my dorm building stood a tiny prayer chapel. The maximum capacity in that thing was probably twenty people, but we would easily squeeze fifty in there on a good night. We would all pile into this little building to worship. Like clockwork, our "spontaneous" gatherings followed a predictable pattern. First, someone would dim the lights (of course), and then everyone would gather close together. One person would be up front, on his knees, gently strumming a guitar. Everyone *obviously* had their eyes closed in silence until, at long last, the guitar player would break into prayer. It usually went something like, "Lord . . . just . . . we just . . . like . . . come to you. Father . . . we want to . . . just . . . like . . . be near you. Just . . . come and . . . just . . . be with us. Draw near to us . . . and just . . . be like . . . present." After a good hour and a half of jamming out together, the leader would end with the same kind of prayer, and we would all exit the tiny chapel with a delirious emotional high.

I'm sure that God was honored by some of our activity. In fact, I can remember specific ways the Lord used those times to minister to my soul. However, so much of what we were doing was flat out wrong. It's that simple. And if anyone is primarily to blame, it's me. I was—more often than not—the fellow up front with the guitar, setting the mood for the entire evening. But I was no lead worshiper; I was a conjurer. I was attempting to summon the presence of God with my repetitive babbling and singing, and his activity in our midst was measured by our emotional barometer.

Here's the problem: the *feeling* I experienced while I was in that tiny chapel is not unique to Christianity. You can get that exact feeling in a multitude of different settings; a tiny building in Southern California is just one of many ways to conjure emotional ecstasy.

THE DECEPTION OF EMOTIONALISM

Did you know that singing releases a chemical in your brain? The chemical is called *dopamine*. It's pretty awesome actually; it's sometimes referred to as the "feel-good chemical," and it's why any sensation is enjoyable. Dopamine is released when certain stimulation occurs; exercising, eating, laughing, singing, even having sex—all of these things are means for releasing dopamine. This is a common design feature that everyone has; it was God's idea to give us this chemical to enable enjoyment of things that should be enjoyed. But sin has a way of perverting all good things, and sin distorts this feel-good chemical by confusion; the gift of dopamine is confused with the Giver. You can see this in the sexually promiscuous and, relevant to the discussion at hand, in the emotionalism that masquerades as true, God-honoring worship.

It's not difficult to imagine how this has happened. We have today a generation of leaders who have been brought up in the church-camp phenomenon. At church camp you typically have a bunch of teenagers unplug from their everyday lives to be immersed in an emphatically Christian context. From early morning until late at night the campers are engaged in reading the Bible, discussing the Bible, praying, singing worship songs, and playing muddy, team-building games. These sorts of experiences tend to leave a mark, especially considering that many of the campers have not grown up in any corporate worship context at all, or they have grown up listening to really "boring" music at their churches. By contrast, the worship band at camp is normally *really* good and *really* engaging. Inevitably, even those kids who were "too cool for school" at the beginning of the week are right there in the front of the crowd by the end of the week, jumping and shouting along with everyone else.

These camps can serve as great spiritual catalysts for the teenagers who go to them. Teens get saved at camp. Teens get called into ministry at camp. Teens get severely convicted of sin and led into genuine repentance at camp. And teens also get really emotional at camp—but often, they don't even know why, and that is a problem. There is a problem when our emotions are stirred without being tethered to any truth.

This is the framework I was working with when I was first given the opportunity to lead worship through song in my church; I had been deeply impacted by a unique experience, and I assumed my role was to recreate the camp environment every Sunday morning. I didn't look for proof texts to justify this notion because my memory *was* the proof text. I could simply say things like, "I *know* God met with me in that environment. Of course I want to give that experience to my congregation!" to which I now respond: "God very well may have met with you in that environment. But he did so according to his divine, sovereign prerogative; he wasn't summoned by the ambiance."

Just because God can use a certain emotionally charged environment to do transformative work doesn't mean that he has prescribed for us to recreate such an environment at every possible opportunity. The distinction between God's "can" and our "should" is significant. The fact that God *can* cause a donkey to speak doesn't mean that we *should* start inviting donkeys to our conferences, for example.

SINCERE(LY WRONG)

The problem is not the feeling. The problem is *chasing* the feeling at all costs, regardless of how we get it. The problem is idolatry. Of course, no Christian would ever *say* that this is what he or she is doing. Every Christian who does this will insist—probably with sincerity—that they are chasing after God, not the feeling (I know I would have insisted as much). But sincerity isn't everything; it is entirely possible to be sincerely wrong. This is exactly why idolatry is so insidiously tricky. Idolatry is simply the act of worshiping anything that is not God. Sometimes this is obvious, like in the case of other religions—a Muslim who engages in worship does not worship the one true God of the universe and is therefore clearly engaged in idolatry. However, sometimes idolatry happens unintentionally by attempting to worship God in an inappropriate manner or by worshiping him for characteristics he doesn't actually have.

Think back on the Israelites' first major rebellion after the Exodus. You remember the scene: God powerfully delivers his people from the Egyptians and sends Moses up to Mount Sinai to give him the law. While Moses is gone, the Israelites get the itch to worship something, and so rather than being a faithful leader, Aaron pampers their depravity. After the golden calf is built—or, after it jumps out of the fire, as Aaron insisted—the people don't say, "This is your *new* God, since we're done with the one who brought us out of Egypt!" No, they say, "behold, the gods *who brought you* out of the land of Egypt." In other words, they attributed the *work of God*—their deliverance from slavery—to this nauseating hunk of metal. In fact, Aaron would go so far as to proclaim a feast to the LORD (that is, Yahweh, Israel's covenant-making, covenant-keeping God) in honor of this thing (Exodus 32:1–6). By worshiping God for characteristics that he did not have, they were not worshiping God at all; they were worshiping an idol—a god made in their image. We often do the same with our worship gatherings. The difference is we are much more cunning.

One of the ways we cater to our idolatry in corporate worship is with ambiguous song lyrics. Ambiguity in corporate worship is dangerous; it's one of the devil's favorite schemes for sneaking pitiful little idols into the worship gatherings of the Almighty.

Let me give you an example. Say the congregation is singing a song with vague, ambiguous lyrics, something along the lines of, "Jesus, you make me feel so good. To you I'm understood. Thank you for wanting me to be happy. You just make me feel all sappy." Now, you can have two people singing this song, side-by-side, with two entirely different activities going on in their hearts, and the ambiguity of the lyrics legitimizes both. What is meant by, "thank you for wanting me to be happy"? Do we mean, "thank you for calling me to yourself, where I can forsake lesser loves to find fullness of joy and pleasure forevermore" (Ps 16:11)? Or, might we mean, "thank you for affirming me without qualification and not caring about my immoral habits, since they make me happy"? The difference matters. One is worship, one is idolatry, but the ambiguous lyrics allow for both interpretations.

Let's get concrete with a real example. One popular contemporary song takes a line from 2 Corinthians 3:17, "where the Spirit of the Lord is, there is freedom," as the main thrust of the song. In the context of the 1 Corinthians, the "freedom" Paul describes is very specific: a freedom from the veil that remains over the face of those who read the Old Testament law apart from Christ. In this passage liberty is defined for us as having a Christocentric understanding of the Old Testament; it is the ability to see the glorious face of Jesus in the text so as to be transformed from one degree of glory to another (2 Cor 3:12–18). However, the song ignores this context. Instead we find: "Freedom reigns in this place / Showers of mercy and grace / Falling on every face / There is freedom."[1] Ambiguous lyrics that rhyme "place" with "grace" and "face" in a haphazard, senseless fashion. Evidently, having coherence in lyrics isn't important for many of our churches; content has taken a back seat. Lying behind this development in evangelicalism is a fundamental misunderstanding of what we're trying to do when we gather together.

BROTHERS, WE ARE NOT CONJURERS

If we're after emotional ecstasy, then lyrics are unimportant. It doesn't matter if the content of our songs is nonsensical because by the twelfth time we sing it we have created the emotive environment we've been striving for. Bob Kauflin is helpful on this: "We need to understand that when words are combined with music we can be deceived. Music can make shallow lyrics sound deep. A great rhythm section can make drivel sound profound and make you want to sing it again."[2] This is true. We can fool ourselves into thinking that what we are doing is right because *something* is happening. But we need to come to terms with the fact that just because *something* is happening, that doesn't mean that God is pleased with it. That something might be a stench in God's nostrils. Just ask Nadab and Abihu what good intentions divorced from faithfulness to God's Word in worship produces (see Leviticus 10). Our impulse should not be to pursue a feeling at any cost; that's not our role as music leaders. We are not conjurers. We are not summoning the Spirit of God.

This is important because it guards against the erroneous notion that the corporate gathering is intended to be fundamentally private. It isn't.

Somehow we've gotten the impression that a Sunday morning service is supposed to be a time for a bunch of people to come into the same room in order to ignore one another.

Our confusion as evangelicals on this particular issue can be attributed to a number of factors, at least one of which is a misapplication of a core doctrines of Christianity that the Protestant Reformation recovered in the sixteenth and seventeenth centuries. The doctrine of justification by grace alone through faith alone rightly undermined the commonly held Roman Catholic notion that churchy activity—sacraments that elicited the approval of the religious arbiters, and therefore the approval of God—is required to secure eternal salvation. The Reformers demolished this "innocent by association" concept of salvation by retrieving the beautiful doctrine of justification by grace alone through faith alone. The Puritans then came along and carried this thinking through to a recovery of personal regeneration.

We evangelicals have rightly received this emphasis from the Reformers. What we have largely *not* received from the Reformers, however, is a confessional understanding of the body of Christ that emphasizes the corporate element of Christianity; we have squandered this element of our heritage. What the Reformers understood—and what evangelicals often miss—is that Christianity is not a purely personal religion. To be sure, the church is comprised of individuals who have been *personally* regenerated by the Holy Spirit and have been justified by grace through faith *individually*, but they have been individually brought into a *corporate* assembly.

That individuals would thrive in solitary Christianity is completely foreign to the New Testament; in fact, it's oxymoronic. To be a Christian is to be part of the church. The common pattern in our churches of turning down the lights and turning up the music so that only the band can be seen and heard is telling; it highlights our misunderstanding of this very foundational aspect of Christianity. We want to forget that there are other people around us (or we want them to be transformed into a nameless, faceless mass—a crowd). But the corporate gathering of the local church is for corporate participation and corporate edification; it's not intended as a time to set up cubicles for secluded emotional experiences. We don't gather together to ignore one another.

"MORE IN THE MONITORS, PLEASE"

Please don't hear me say that low lights and loud music are intrinsically wrong. Later on, I will argue that forms of music and methodology are not neutral, but for now all I want to do is shine a spotlight on intentions. Why are we making *these* sorts of aesthetic tweaks to the corporate worship service? Why low lights? Why loud music? I just described one motivation, namely, the motivation to create holy cubicles where individuals in the congregation can tune everyone else out to have their own secluded, private moments with God. There is also another reason for creating this kind of environment, and it's no less individualistic: the music leader may be a big 'ol showboat.

Even if it's not glaringly obvious, every music leader stares this reality in the face. We all have these kinds of thoughts whiz through our minds: "What do people think of me? Will they like this part of the song? Did they notice when I did that? Do they like my singing? Do they think I'm good? How can I get a good reaction out of them?" These are the thoughts of a performer. So what should we do with them? Should we entertain them or slay them? Should we justify them or strangle them? I should like to think that asking the question is answering it; most people will agree that these questions don't reflect the music leader's role and that they should be repented of and discarded. However, the problem isn't how these man-fearing, ego-stroking thoughts should be addressed when they're noticed; the problem is that they aren't often noticed at all! But if we do a little reverse engineering with certain elements of our worship gathering, I think we'll find these questions at the root. We want the music loud *because* we want to be heard. We turn the lights down on everything except the stage *because* we want to be seen. To put it simply, we turn the corporate worship gathering into a rock concert *because we want to be rock stars.*

This kind of individualism is the worst of all because it reduces the congregation of God's blood-bought children to a mere audience. The music leader uses the corporate gathering as a platform for his own vanity, and the service is made into nothing more than a concert—an opportunity to showcase his talents. I speak from experience when I say that this kind of manipulation is illusive—the music leader can disregard any accusation of it by pointing to the happy faces and enthusiastic compliments of his fans, "How can I be accused of using them when they're clearly having a great time?" But this kind of influential abuse is a slow and steady poison. The music leader gets all the enjoyments of being a rock star, and the congregation gets all the enjoyments of going to a rock show, while both parties are being deprived of humble, corporate, God-honoring expressions of worship through song. Everyone loses.

If you take nothing else away from this chapter, my dear reader, remember that the people of God who gather together on Sunday mornings are not there to hear you sing, and you're not there to show off your talent. Your skills are not trophies to display; they are tools to use. The music leader is not an entertainer.

CHAPTER 2

REVELATION AND RESPONSE

What do we even mean when we say *worship*? Our word *worship* has come from the Old English word, *weorthscipe*—or *worth*-ship, if you like. Fundamentally, to worship is to ascribe worth to something or someone. No one actually needs to be taught how to worship; we are constantly making judgment calls, ascribing value to things we consider worthy of commendation or praise. This is a design feature we all have. God has wired humans such that we are driven to look for greatness and to ascribe worth to it when it is found. We tell people about our favorite bands because we consider their music worthy of the enjoyment of others; we are praising them. We tell people about our favorite restaurants because we have tasted and seen that their food is good, and we feel the need to ascribe worth to them.

Worship is comprised of two essential elements: revelation and response. *Revelation* gives us the motivation to worship, and our response is the expression of our worship. Imagine walking into a newly discovered cafe to find that this particular establishment roasts the best coffee in the entire world; that's revelation. Now imagine going back to all of your coffee-snob friends and telling them about it; that's response. Revelation and response: this is how worship fundamentally works.

For worship to be appropriate, response needs to fittingly correspond to the object that has been revealed. If we are worshiping one thing and we discover something else with value surpassing the thing we are currently worshiping, it would not be appropriate to go on worshiping the inferior object over against the superior one. To borrow an analogy from C.S. Lewis, it wouldn't be right to prefer playing with mud pies in the city slums over a trip to the beach. That which has surpassing value ought to be regarded as such.

REVELATION: WHO IS GOD?

It stands to reason that if something, or someone, is more valuable than anything else in the universe, that thing or person ought to be the absolute and ultimate object of our worship. So what would qualify someone as being that valuable? What credentials would he need to have? *Would speaking the universe into existence do?*

Only God surpasses all else in worth. He alone deserves our ultimate worship. Who is this preeminent object of all worship? 'Let's pause and reflect on what God has revealed about himself.

God Is. Before time began, there was God, enjoying the perfect community of himself: Father, Son, and Holy Spirit. He needed nothing. He was eternally sufficient in himself; he never felt lonely, he never felt confused, he never felt lack of any kind—only the pure enjoyment of his own perfection. "Heaven is my throne," he says, "and the earth is my footstool; what is the house that you would build for me, and what is the place of my rest?" (Isa 66:1) He is the "I AM" (Exod 3:14), Alpha and the Omega, the beginning and the end (Rev 1:8). God is worthy of our worship because he is the great, Triune, personal absolute; he stands over and above everything. He is perfect in every way, and he exists according to his own intrinsic self-sufficiency.

God is Lord of Creation. God is absolutely sovereign over all creation. He spoke the universe into existence (Gen 1:3–30, John 1:1–5, Col 1:15–20). The same Word who created everything from nothing is the Word who currently sustains the universe with his power (Heb 1:1–3). This means God's lack of involvement wouldn't just be unfortunate for the universe; it would mean the loss of the universe's own existence. Nothing in the universe has absolute autonomy; everything that is not God is essentially dependent on God, which basically means God is a glorious micromanager. He leaves nothing alone. The universe isn't a lifeless machine God created to operate automatically and stepped away from; the cogs of the cosmos are continually turning because *God tells them to*.

Understand what this implies: everything—every single thing—belongs to him. He is the master of all things! Listen to the Psalmist: "By the word of the Lord the heavens were made, and by the breath of his mouth all their host. He gathers the waters of the sea as a heap; he puts the deeps in storehouses. Let all the earth fear the Lord; let all the inhabitants of the world stand in awe of him! For he spoke, and it came to be; he commanded, and it stood firm. (Ps 33:6–9)"

Make no mistake, all of nature is under God's dominion. Think about the beauty of the natural universe: billions of stars, breathed out effortlessly by the Almighty. How many birds exist on this planet? How many creatures of the sea? How many animals in the wilderness? How many insects crawling around in the grass outside your window right now? How many molecules comprise every one of those creatures, operating with very specific job descriptions? And *how* did all of this stuff get here? This one time, God said, "Let there be."

I love the way N. D. Wilson puts it in *Notes from the Tilt-A-Whirl*: "We have given them names, shortcutting them with smaller sounds, sounds that fit in our mouths. Tree, I say, and you know what I mean. You see one in your mind, or glace out your window and remember the much-needed pruning. Tree, God says, and there is one. But He doesn't say the word *tree*; He says the tree itself. He needs no shortcut. He's not merely calling one into existence, though His voice creates. His voice *is* its existence."[3]

Everything that exists finds its origin in the sovereign Word of God. And everything that exists is bragging about it! "The heavens declare the glory of God and the sky above proclaims his handiwork. Day to day pours out speech and night to night reveals knowledge." (Ps 19:1–2) The lordship that God demonstrates in creating and sustaining everything demands that he be worshiped.

God is Lord of History. Not only is God sovereign over the affairs of amoral nature; the course of human history is also under his lordship. He can never be thwarted by the will of man (Ps 33:13–19); he does what he pleases (Ps 115:3). Kingdoms rise and fall according to his purposes. "The king's heart is a stream of water in the hand of the Lord," we are told, "he turns it *wherever* he will." (Prov 21:1) Human history isn't incidental; God is telling a story. It is a glorious story that we will discuss in further detail later, but for now it is sufficient to say that God is worthy of worship because he is the grand, storytelling Lord of history.

God is after his Glory. If you've never thought about this before, it might be surprising for you to notice how God-centered God is. The ultimate end for everything he does is his own glory. All throughout Scripture we find passages like Isaiah 45:22–23: "Turn to me and be saved, all the ends of the earth! For I am God, and there is no other. By myself I have sworn; from my mouth has gone out righteousness a word that shall not return; 'To me every knee shall bow, every tongue shall swear allegiance.'"

Here we see that God intends even his grace in saving to conclude with bowed knees and affirmations of allegiance. That's *why* he saves by grace. This point is more clearly accentuated in Isaiah 48, where God speaks through his prophet to declare, "For my name's sake I defer my anger, for the sake of my praise I restrain it for you, that I may not cut you off. Behold, I have refined you, but not as silver; I have tried you in the furnace of affliction. For my own sake, for my own sake, I do it, for how should my name be profaned? My glory I will not give to another." (Isa 48:9–11)

This may upset our sensibilities, but it shouldn't. Isn't it right to ascribe praise to that which is supremely worthy of praise? Is there anything in existence that is more deserving of worship besides God? It would be inappropriate for God to be pleased with glorifying anything besides himself, because anything besides himself is infinitely inferior to himself! Understand this very important truth: God is after his glory, and he will get it.

Christian worship, therefore, starts with a revelation of an enormous God, a God who would remain supremely glorious whether or not we ever acknowledge him. C. S. Lewis said it vividly, "A man can no more diminish God's glory by refusing to worship Him than a lunatic can put out the sun by scribbling 'darkness' on the walls of his cell."[4]

What's jarring about all of this is that even God's love for us is subservient to his love for his own glory. In other words, he shows grace to his creatures *because* that grace contributes to his purpose of being glorified. "In love he predestined us for adoption as sons through Jesus Christ," Paul tells us, "according to the purpose of his will," why does he do this? ". . . *to the praise of his glorious grace*" (Eph 1:5–6). I understand that this flies right in the face of many of the man-centered songs we sing in church today, but so what? Let the chips fall where they may; worship of the Ancient of Days, in spirit and in truth, can only happen when we see how dreadfully awesome he truly is, and one of the things that makes him dreadfully awesome is his commitment to glorify himself.

RESPONSE: WE WORSHIP FOR A REASON

In light of all this revelation, we respond with worship. Worship can't start with us; it *must* start with God. Once we behold this massive, Triune God, worship becomes a natural response. This may sound like an obvious progression, but often our worship services don't reflect this logical order. So often we try to move straight to the affections rather than the mind. This is unhealthy' and unbiblical. In Scripture *knowledge* always stirs *affection*. Our worship has a reason.

Consider Paul's sudden burst into doxology at the end of Romans 11: "Oh, the depth of the riches and wisdom and knowledge of God! How unsearchable are his judgments and how inscrutable his ways!" (v. 33) What could have possibly led to such an "Oh"? Theology, that's what! Paul had just concluded an eleven-chapter-long train of thought. It was one, consistent, complex argument, connecting one clause to another, packed with more theological insight than perhaps any other portion of Scripture. *That* is what elicited Paul's "Oh!"

Look also to the Psalms. You will never find a psalm in the Bible that doesn't give an explicit reason for worshipping God. "Ascribe to the Lord the glory due his name; worship the Lord in the splendor of holiness." Why? Because "The voice of the Lord is over the waters; the God of glory thunders, the Lord, over many waters" (Ps 29:2–3). "Enter his gates with thanksgiving, and his courts with praise! Give thanks to him; bless his name!" Why? "For the Lord is good; his steadfast love endures forever, and his faithfulness to all generations" (Ps 100:4–5). "Sing praises to God, sing praises! Sing praises to our King, sing praises!" Why? "For God is the King of all the earth; sing praises with a psalm" (Ps 47:6–7). God doesn't want our thoughtless, mushy emotionalism; he is a self-disclosing God for a reason. He has communicated to us with the book of creation and the book of his holy, inerrant, inspired words; and it is in light of this *information* that he desires to be praised.

Understand that this in no way diminishes the importance of emotion. We would be right to critique cold, indifferent declarations of orthodox doctrine, but we would be dead wrong to assume that serious, intellectually stimulating meditation on Scripture will automatically produce orthodustiness. To the contrary, right thinking of God causes our emotional engagement to deepen. When we focus on the grandeur of God's actual glory, we are freed from superficial stimulation of our emotions; we can rest assured, knowing that our vision of God—rather than our pitiful effort of emotion conjuring—compels us to worship. This is how we safeguard authenticity in our worship: we think hard on God's nature and character.

Let me say one more thing about emotions before we move on. Recall the previous chapter, when I said that dopamine is released in our brains when we sing, and we should therefore watch out for the propensity to manipulate our emotions to *feel* like we're worshiping Go, when in reality we are merely experiencing the natural effects of a particular physical activity. I must hasten to add that we should not be afraid of experiencing this natural feeling when we are singing truth. We *should* enjoy that "feel-good chemical" in its proper context. God made our brains to work that way on purpose; and it's with this awareness that he *commands* us to sing in Scripture.

We need to be willing to worship God with our whole beings; it is impossible to detach our spiritual worship from physical involvement, and we should never even try. "There is no good trying to be more spiritual than God." C. S. Lewis reminds us, "God never meant man to be a purely spiritual creature. That is why He uses material things like bread and wine to put the new life into us. We may think this rather crude and unspiritual. God does not: He invented eating. He likes matter. He invented it."[5]

THE GOSPEL AS FUEL FOR WORSHIP

I said earlier that God deserves to be worshiped because he is the grand, storytelling Lord of history. So what story is he telling? The gospel. From the beginning of time to eternity after the resurrection, history is telling a narrative; there is a beginning, a catastrophe, a climax, and a resolution. In this story we see mystery and conflict, tragedy and victory, surprise twists and irony. There are many villains in this story, and there is a hero—his name is Jesus.

The gospel is the center of the Bible, and it is the center of human history. We are told in Romans 3:21–26 that all of the saints before the incarnation were looking forward to the cross for their justification, and all of the saints following Jesus' ascension are looking back to the cross for their justification. History has a gravitational pull toward Calvary.

One of my favorite passages, which illustrates the climax of this story, is found Philippians 2:

> Have this mind among yourselves, which is yours in Christ Jesus, who, though he was in the form of God, did not count equality with God a thing to be grasped, but emptied himself, by taking the form of a servant, being born in the likeness of men. And being found in human form, he humbled himself by becoming obedient to the point of death, even death on a cross. Therefore God has highly exalted him and bestowed on him the name that is above every name, so that at the name of Jesus every knee should bow, in heaven and on earth and under the earth, and every tongue confess that Jesus Christ is Lord, to the glory of God the Father. (Phil 2:5–11)

A story can't get better than this! The Author actually *wrote himself into* his own story in order to save his characters from their peril. The hero of the story actually defeated his enemies by uniting himself to them, crucifying them in him, burying them in the grave, and resurrecting them—now no longer as his enemies but as his friends (Gal 2:20; Rom 5:10; 6:4; 2 Cor 5:21).

There is no better fuel for worship than the gospel. In fact, the gospel is what gives us the possibility of worshiping rightly at all. We cannot worship God if there is hostility between us and God, and in the gospel we find reconciliation (2 Cor 5:18–21). We cannot worship God if we are trapped in the domain of darkness, and in the gospel we are transferred into the kingdom of his beloved Son (Col 1:13–14). We cannot worship God if we are dead in our trespasses, and in the gospel we are made alive together with him (Eph 2:1–10). In the gospel we are the adopted children of God, a kingdom of priests, a chosen people, the beloved of God. The only appropriate response to such grace is worship.

By the way, this is exactly why the corporate gatherings of God's people shouldn't be tailored toward attracting unbelievers; none of these gratitude-inducing realities are true for them. They are still dead in their trespasses. But even if they *could* worship God, they wouldn't want to; God displays his glory in the cross, and to the perishing the cross is a stumbling block and foolishness (1 Cor 1:18–25). They can't worship God for the glory of the cross because they *don't consider it glorious.*

John MacArthur said it potently: "More to the point, there is no warrant in Scripture for adapting the church's weekly gatherings to the preferences of unbelievers. Indeed, the practice seems contrary to the spirit of everything Scripture says about the assembly of believers. When the church comes together on the Lord's Day is no time to entertain the lost, amuse the brethren, or otherwise cater to the 'felt needs' of those in attendance. This is when we should bow before our God as a congregation and honor Him with our worship."[6]

Unbelievers are bound to be present in our gatherings, and we should acknowledge their presence and welcome them. They need the gospel, and they should find it at our meetings. But the corporate gathering isn't *for* them. They will come and see what Christians do, and they will see and hear the gospel displayed and proclaimed, and it will transform them. But when they come, their comfort should not be a dictating concern for us. Who *wants* to hear that they're filthy sinners in need of grace? That's uncomfortable for the unbeliever, and if their comfort is paramount for us, we won't cut them with the sword of the Spirit. If the comfort of the unbeliever is our primary concern, then the believers will be starving themselves of true worship, the cross will be robbed of its power, the unbeliever will go without hearing the gospel, and God will not be honored. Everyone loses in that scenario.

Let's also note that such an approach to worship necessitates that our corporate worship be *trinitarian*. We come to God the Father in worship by virtue of the power of God the Holy Spirit, who is our helper, purchased for us by the blood of God the Son. It is impossible to relate to God outside of a trinitarian framework, not only because he *is* Trinity (so relating to God outside of a trinitarian framework isn't actually relating to *God*), but also because everything he does (including his act of saving us) is trinitarian. When we therefore respond to his triune revelation, our response should be trinitarian in some way (more on this later).

At this point we need to address the necessity of corporate gatherings. After all, many of the benefits of the gospel just mentioned are very personal. *I'm* grateful that I have been brought from death to life, because I know where I would be if I were still dead in *my* trespasses. Even now while I'm typing this sentence, thinking about these glorious realities, I'm moved with gratitude and adoration; the *click click click* of this keyboard is the sound of my worship! So if we can (and should) worship God individually and in different ways, what is the point of a corporate gathering?

We have already established that God's intended end of all that he does is his own glory, and he glorifies himself in a number of ways. When he breathed the universe into existence, the angelic host sang his praises (Job 38:7); in this, he was being glorified. As we've already seen, creation *itself* speaks of its Master's handiwork and thereby glorifies him (Ps 19:1–6). We see in Scripture that God glorifies himself by judging the wicked (Ps 21:9–13), and yet he also glorifies himself by showing mercy on his people (Isa 48:9–11). In all of this God is magnificently glorious. However, there is one display of his divine power that makes all of his other works pale in comparison. It is called the church.

A BRIEF BIBLICAL THEOLOGY OF THE CHURCH

The Bible calls the church a "mystery." To understand the full weight of this mystery, we need to do a little biblical theology. Before Christ came in the flesh, the average Jew would have never conceived of such a thing as the church (namely, a meshing of all kinds of people, enjoying the blessings of God); God's people were the Israelites. Ethnic identity was everything. If you were a Jew, you were an heir to the promises of God; if you were a Gentile, you were not. Plain and simple. That is how the people of God would have understood the nature of the world at the time. And what we need to understand about the Old Testament is that God did in fact choose Israel to be his peculiar people among the nations. However, the blessings of God were never meant to stay exclusively with Israel. Israel was always meant to be a funnel through which the promises of God could be extended to the nations. The saints of old couldn't have known how exactly this would work out, but occasionally God threw a wrench in the spokes of their ethnocentric wheels with passages like Isaiah 19:24–25, which says that Israel will be *third*, along with Assyria and Egypt. They would have been flabbergasted at passages like that! Nevertheless, it has always been in the mind of God to bless peoples of all nations, not merely the people of Israel. And God's intended means for dispensing these blessings to the nations is the gospel.

Think back on Genesis 3, when the gospel was promised for the very first time in human history. Right after Adam and Eve's initial disobedience, God makes this declaration to the serpent: "I will put enmity between you and the woman, and between your offspring and her offspring; he shall bruise your head, and you shall bruise his heel." (Gen 3:15) This single offspring would crush the head of Satan, bringing reconciliation between man and God once more.

As we move down through history, we see this promise narrowing from being an offspring of Eve (which qualifies every human being in all of human history besides Adam), to being more specifically an offspring of Abraham (Gen 12:1–9), and then of Isaac (Gen 26:4–5), and finally of Jacob (Gen 28:13). Jacob fathered the nation of Israel, but the narrowing lens of history still hadn't focused on this "offspring" just yet. It went from Israel (Jacob) to Judah (Gen 49:10), from the line of Judah to David (1 Sam 16:1–13), and eventually from the line of David to Jesus (Matt 1:1–17).

So this promised offspring, mentioned all the way back in Genesis 3, is Jesus. Paul says this explicitly in Galatians 3: "Now the promises were made to Abraham and to his offspring. It does not say, 'And to your offsprings,' referring to many, but referring to one, 'And to your offspring,' who is Christ" (Gal 3:16). So far this really isn't a problem with the first-century Jewish conception of God's promises. After all, Jesus is from the tribe of Judah. The promises are still being kept for the Jews, right? Wrong. Before he says this in Galatians, Paul explains how in Jesus

Christ, the blessings of Abraham would come, not only to the Jews, but to the Gentiles through faith (Gal 3:13–14).

This is the idea: the promises of God are for the offspring of Abraham—namely, Jesus—and those who are united to him by faith, share those same promises. The beautiful thing is that the only prerequisite for being united to this offspring of Abraham is faith. Whether one is a Jew or a Greek, a slave or a free person, a male or a female, any kind of person can become united to Christ by faith and thereby receive all the promises of God (Gal 3:28).

This may not seem like a big deal to us, but to the first-century world it was jarring. Paul called it a mystery—that is, it was hidden but now it's revealed—that Gentiles are fellow heirs, "members of the same body, partakers of the promise in Christ Jesus through the gospel" (Eph 3:6). Before Christ there were two men: the Jew and the Gentile—the one near to the promises of God and the other far off. There was hostility between these two men; they had no business being in the same room together. But when Christ Jesus came, he tore down the dividing wall of hostility between the two men and he created from them—in himself—one new man (Eph 2:11–22).

GOD'S MASTERPIECE

The church, therefore, is God's masterpiece. Paul describes this great work thoroughly in this passage to the Ephesian Church:

> Of this gospel I was made a minister according to the gift of God's grace, which was given me by the working of his power. To me, though I am the very least of all the saints, this grace was given, to preach to the Gentiles the unsearchable riches of Christ, and to bring to light for everyone

> what is the plan of the mystery hidden for ages in God who created all things, so that through the church the manifold wisdom of God might now be made known to the rulers and authorities in the heavenly places. This was according to the eternal purpose that he has realized in Christ Jesus our Lord, in whom we have boldness and access with confidence through our faith in him. So I ask you not to lose heart over what I am suffering for you, which is your glory. For this reason I bow my knees before the Father, from whom every family in heaven and on earth is named, that according to the riches of his glory he may grant you to be strengthened with power through his Spirit in your inner being, so that Christ may dwell in your hearts through faith—that you, being rooted and grounded in love, may have strength to comprehend with all the saints what is the breadth and length and height and depth, and to know the love of Christ that surpasses knowledge, that you may be filled with all the fullness of God. Now to him who is able to do far more abundantly that all that we ask or think, according to the power at work within us, to him be glory in the church and in Christ Jesus throughout all generations, forever and ever. Amen. (Eph 3:7–21)

This passage lays out not only what the church is but also what she does and why she exists. The "manifold wisdom of God" is not seen in his ability to create everything from nothing; his manifold wisdom—the absolute apex of his glory—is seen in the *church*. In the creation of the cosmos, the angels sang with joy. In creation of the church, their jaws drop from amazement (Eph 3:10, 1 Pet 1:12).

The key to understanding Ephesians 2 is to identify the construction language; the "breadth and length and height and depth" are measurements of a building. This is a multifaceted, multicolored building, comprised of material that is not supposed to fit together. Like a mosaic, God takes pieces of seemingly irreconcilable origin and constructs a work of dazzling brilliance! He is a master builder, and his masterpiece—his most prized work—is the church. *This* is where his glory is most magnified. So now we have an answer to our question.

Question: Why gather corporately as a church to glorify God?

Answer: Because that is where he is most glorified.

This point should caution us from individualistic navel gazing. We were created to glorify God, and his primary means of getting glory is through the church, not our rogue efforts. We should therefore not think that our privileged involvement in this grand purpose of existence can be adequately experienced outside the regular gatherings of the church. We don't truly want to see God glorified if we neglect to participate in what brings him the most glory.

TEACHING AND ADMONISHING

To worship God corporately because it brings him glory is a great motivation as it is; we were created to worship him, and fulfilling the purpose of our existence is a sweet thing. But is there anything else we can look forward to in corporate worship? In other words, is our only gift in worshiping God the satisfaction of doing what we were created to do, or are there other benefits as well? God could have just said, "Worship me corporately because I made you to glorify me, that's how I'm most glorified," and that would be enough. But God has so graciously sweetened the deal.

Notice Paul's instructions to the Colossians:

> Put on then, as God's chosen ones, holy and beloved, compassionate hearts, kindness, humility, meekness, and patience, bearing with one another and, if one has a complaint against another, forgiving each other; as the Lord has forgiven you, so you also must forgive. And above all these put on love, which binds everything together in perfect harmony. And let the peace of Christ rule in your hearts, to which indeed you were called in one body. And be thankful. Let the word of Christ dwell in you richly, teaching and admonishing one another in all wisdom, singing psalms and hymns and spiritual songs, with thankfulness in your hearts to God. And whatever you do, in word or deed, do everything in the name of the Lord Jesus, giving thanks to God the Father through him. (Col 3:12–17)

This passage tells us to get close to other Christians—close enough to need patience and humility and forgiveness. We are told to get so close it hurts. Notice, we aren't told to come together merely to enjoy each other's company; we have a rally cry, and it is our devotion to Christ, who rules in our hearts. It's no coincidence that the instruction to let the word of Christ dwell in us richly is mentioned in the same breath as the instruction to sing psalms, hymns, and spiritual songs. Paul is endorsing Christ-centered, Christ-exalting worship. Why? Because that's how the Church is built up. We see this especially in chapter 2, when Paul warns the Colossians against straying away into worship of angels and obsessive attention to visions in contrast to "holding fast to the Head, from whom the whole body, nourished and knit together through its joints and ligaments, grows with a growth that is from God" (Col 2:19) This is crucial. Paul states emphatically that God grows his church when its members cling to Christ.

So we're told to let the word of Christ dwell in us richly when we sing, in such a way that we teach and admonish one another in all wisdom. What exactly does that look like? At the very least it means that our songs are substantial enough *to teach us something*. This doesn't necessarily mean that our songs must have a minimum word count of one thousand, nor does it mean that our songs must be hymns. Some of the most profound songs are simple and easy to remember. However, the songs must be saying *something*. They shouldn't be ambiguous or nonsensical. We should be clearly praising God for things that are true of him.

Not only does "teaching and admonishing" imply that our Christ-exalting songs ought to have significant content, it also implies much about the way we interact with one another. When we bear with one another in community, it will certainly impact how we worship in our corporate gatherings. When I see the mother of a three-year-old, cancer-stricken little girl, raising her hands in adoration, singing a song of praise to God for his sovereign goodness, I am being taught. When I see a father who has just been laid off from work zealously thanking God for his provision, I am being taught. There is so much edification that comes along with this kind of unity. But here's the rub: we can't benefit from this kind of edification if we're not intimately knit together in love. Unless I know that a three-year-old is battling cancer, the raised hands of her mother will mean nothing to me. We can't share in profound joy with one another unless we're willing to share in profound pain as well.

I'm reminded of a young woman in a community group I used to be a part of who constantly ached for her drug-worn mother. Nearly every week, while the group shared prayer needs, she melted into sobs upon the mention of her mom. I remember one week in particular, she was brave enough to admit, "I know this sounds awful, but I'm so exhausted by my mother that I don't even want to think about her or pray for her." In moments like that, the great privilege is given to her faith community to respond with, "Alright then, we will pray for her *on your behalf*." That's intercession. That's what it means to bear with one another; it means to come alongside those in your midst who have fallen under the weight of their burdens to share the load.

When this kind of intimacy is present in the body, God does an amazing thing. Paul describes this in 2 Corinthians: "Blessed be the God and Father of our Lord Jesus Christ, the Father of mercies and God of all comfort, who comforts us in all our affliction, that we may be able to comfort those who are in any affliction, with the comfort with which we ourselves are comforted by God" (2 Cor 1:3–4).

Did you catch that? Paul says, "God comforts us, so that we can comfort others." *Whose comfort are you comforting others with, Paul?* "That would be God's." This is amazing, isn't it? God comforts his people *through the comfort* of his people. I know what a hug from God feels like because I have experienced it through the mediating arms of a fellow church member. I know what the reassuring words of God sound like because they have been spoken to me through brothers and sisters in Christ who administer Scripture-saturated promises as fellow priests of a holy nation (1 Pet 2:12).

In 2 Corinthians 7 this point is made breathtakingly clear: "But God, who comforts the downcast, comforted us by the coming of Titus, and not only by his coming but also by the comfort with which he was comforted by you, as he told us of your longing, your mourning, your zeal for me, so that I rejoiced still more" (2 Cor 7:6–7).

God comforted Paul by Titus. But not only that, God also comforted Titus through the Corinthians. And, amazingly enough, God comforted Paul through the Corinthians comforting Titus! In other words, Paul was comforted by God vicariously through the comfort that the Corinthians gave Titus. So God speaks through his people, to his people. There are things that God intends to do in our lives, and he has ordained to do them through the people in our churches.

I understand that being close with other Christians is difficult. After all, one of God's specialties is placing people together who would usually never have anything to do with one another. Often a love for Jesus is the only thing we have in common with the other members of our church, but that is plenty. God wants us to experience this kind of messy community when we come together in worship. He is honored by it. All of this implies that our worship—even our corporate worship—must necessarily consist of more than our Sunday morning gatherings. This is precisely where we are going in the next chapter.

CHAPTER 3

VERTICAL DAILY WORSHIP

The role of a music leader is simple: invite the congregation to do what he is doing. If you are going to invite your people to see and savor Jesus, you must be seeing and savoring him.[7] If you are going to invite your people to be humbled by the awesome might of God displayed in his creation, then you must be humbly awestruck by the might of God displayed in his creation. Therefore, the life of a musical-worship leader should be marked by habitual worship such that the corporate gathering on Sunday morning is the apex of a doxological week. This is true of all Christians, but it is especially true for those who are responsible for leading God's people in corporate worship.

In the last chapter I said that human beings are wired to be worshipers; we are never *not* worshiping. We cannot ever flip the "adoration" switch in our brains off, and we should not want to. The problem the gospel fixes is not that we don't worship; the problem the gospel fixes is that we don't worship *God*. So how do we do this outside of our corporate gathering? What does it look like on Monday through Saturday? These next two chapters explore what personal, daily worship looks like.

WAKING UP TO THE SONG

So where do we start? One basic way for us to be compelled to worship God in our daily lives is by simply waking up to creation's daily worship of God. Psalm 19 is a tremendous help to that end: "The heavens declare the glory of God, and the sky above proclaims his handiwork. Day to day pours out speech, and night to night reveals knowledge. There is no speech, nor are there words, whose voice is not heard. In them he has set a tent for the sun, which comes out like a bridegroom leaving his chamber and, like a strong man, runs its course with joy. It's rising is from the end of the heavens, and its circuit to the end of them, and there is nothing hidden from its heat" (Ps 19:1–6).

In the last chapter I mentioned that this Psalm describes how creation brags on God. "Check us out!" say the heavens, "We are the handiwork of God Almighty! We are what his *doodling* looks like!" And we would be wise to listen. When we are shaken from our introspective, egomaniacal, self-absorbed daydream by the loud shouts of creation, profound adoration wells up within our souls. It's a song that causes us to say, "Whoa, a human being, who used to not *exist*, just came out of my wife." or "Whoa, taste buds are actually a thing." or "Whoa, I have a body that runs automatic maintenance to self-heal my bumps and bruises." In other words, wonder yields worship.

I love how N. D. Wilson tries to slap his readers out of lethargic indifference with regard to this wonder

> I've watched goldfish make babies, and ants execute earwigs. I've seen a fly deliver live young while having its head eaten by a mantis. And I had a golden retriever that behaved like one. This is not a sober world. A mouse once pooped on my toddler nephew, provoked by his traps in the living room. Misled by board books, my nephew identified the offending

> rodent as a sheep. Bats really do exist. Caterpillars really turn into butterflies—it's not just a lie for children. Coal squishes into diamonds. Apple trees turn flowers into apples using sunlight and air. I've seen a baby born. And, *ahem*, I know what made it. But I'm not telling. You'd never believe me.[8]

So at least part of what it means to live a life of worship looks like having a bucket of creation's cold water dumped on us to jolt us into an awareness of reality—the reality that "all things were made through [the Word], and without him was not anything made that was made" (John 1:3).

Perhaps I should use an example. Not long ago my wife and I joined my in-laws for a summer vacation. It was a drive-by vacation in which we spent time hiking, mountain biking, and camping in the vast Arches National Park in Utah, the Grand Canyon in Arizona, the badlands of New Mexico, and the sand dunes of Colorado. It was one of those vacations that leaves you more tired than rested, but all in the best way possible. One night we decided to watch the sunset at a popular location in Arches National Park (which, if you've never been there, is that huge portion of land in Utah filled with bizarre natural red rock formations of arches and towers). So we went to the famously picturesque lookout of delicate arch, a popular arch because it looks like it could topple at any moment. The lookout was located at the end of a cliff, directly in front of a deep chasm, which separated us from the giant cliff on which *delicate arch* rested.

We hiked to the lookout with backpacks full of water and fruit cups, and there we waited. We were ready, like Bilbo and his company of dwarves, anticipating the sun to set through the arch's keyhole. While we waited I looked to my right and noticed that the cliff on which we stood inclined steadily up to a peak. Since no one else ventured to the top, naturally I began to make my way, imagining—pretending, really—that my exploration had the mark of novelty.

As I made my way to the top, I found myself altogether disinterested in watching the sun set through delicate arch; at this point I was too high to see that sight, and the scene I now beheld at the peak of that mountain trumped the postcard image of the arch anyway. I stood there, alone, gorging myself on the panoramic vistas of cliffs and valleys, backdropped with orange and purple and pink skies. I felt as if it were too indulgent to enjoy the sight by myself; it just *couldn't* have been fair for me to see that unique sunset, from that vantage point, with that gentle chill, feeling that pleasant ache in my feet all alone. Was it right for me to have that flash of history all to myself? The moment would never be recreated. There would be many more would-be adventurers to hike up that peak and gaze at more sunsets, but *that* sunset, at *that* moment, from *that* place was beheld by my eyes *alone*. I'm tempted to say that the sunset was *mine*, but that would be too presumptuous. I knew I was a guest in someone else's home (or someone else's *footstool*).

Standing there, I felt compelled to worship. I felt myself resounding with the words of David, "When I see your heavens, the work of your fingers, the moon and the stars, which you have set in place, what is man that you are mindful of him, or the son of man that you should care for him?" (Ps 8:3–4) So I began to sing, "Oh Lord my God, when I in *awesome wonder*, consider all the worlds thy hands have made . . ." In other words, the siren song of creation was irresistible; I *had* to contribute to the melody of praise! I had to give my "Amen" to creation's chorus, "How great Thou art! How great Thou art!"

CREATION'S CREATION—ART AND THE GLORY OF GOD

But don't think that awaking to creation's song can only happen by fixing our eyes on that which has been created *ex nihilo*. The reality is, God's creativity is magnified not only by his creation but also by his creation's creation. God made man in his image as a little mirror to reflect, with the intention of turning the whole world into a labyrinth of mirrors so that everywhere you look, you see God and his glory. And one of the ways man reflects God is by being like him in creative pursuits. This means that man-made art can—and should, if it's doing its job—awaken you to creation's song in worship.

Music is a great aid for this. One example, for me, is an album by Levi the Poet (who is a spoken-word artist) called *Correspondence: A Fiction*. This little masterpiece is a concept album that tells the story of a scruffy boy in love with the daughter of a whaling captain who takes his little girl out with him on his final voyage. While the girl is away, the boy decides to build a treehouse for them to live in upon her return, and each song on the album is a letter from a correspondence between the girl and the boy sent by sea bottle (with the exception of one song, which is a diary entry of the girl's father).

It's really a simple, childhood love story that doesn't sound too special at the outset, yet within this little narrative Levi is able to embed some of the most profound lyrics I have ever heard to address issues like depression, love, the meaning of beauty, the meaning of suffering, the meaning of loneliness, the meaning of death, the folly of self-vindication, the folly of pride, the folly of lazy and gnostic ethics (that is, the temptation to condemn created things as intrinsically evil), fatherlessness, motherlessness, and redemption. All of these elements are pulled together with fitting music in such a way that the finished product is a work of art that is, in my experience, unparalleled in its genre. It is a piece of art that essentially *preaches*. When I listen to this album—creation's creation; Levi as an image bearer reflecting God's creativity in his own creativity—I am moved to worship. And it's glorious because I'm not moved to worship Levi or his album; instead, I'm moved to worship the God they (both Levi and his album) reflect.

Good literature is another useful artistic tool for catapulting us Godward. One of my favorite examples is C. S. Lewis's *The Great Divorce*, a fictional story about inhabitants of hell (which is called the "grey city") getting on a bus and driving to heaven. The inhabitants of hell are depicted as transparent ghost-like figures who are totally unfit for the harsh landscape of heaven, which is *more* solid and real than earth (just chew on *that* imagery for a minute!). The whole book is basically a series of conversations between these ghost-like inhabitants of hell and the solid inhabitants of heaven (identified as "Spirits"). The imagery in is thick, and Lewis masterfully illustrates concepts like sanctification, pride, suffering, redemption, and the glory of God.

In one of these conversations, a Spirit converses with a Ghost who was a successful painter in her previous life on earth. In the course of the conversation, the Spirit explains the true purpose of artwork: "When you painted on earth—at least in your earlier days—it was because you caught glimpses of Heaven in the earthly landscape. The success of your painting was that it enabled others to see the glimpses too. . . . Light itself was your first love: you loved paint only as a means of telling about light."[9]

For me, Lewis's own artistic pursuit (specifically, the book from where this excerpt is taken) does just this for me; it illustrates the glory of God and points me heavenward. Good artwork, at its best, does this. It doesn't ultimately point to itself, but rather beyond itself to the absolute origin of beauty, and art *par excellence*: The Triune God himself!

RESETTING DAILY

So part of what it means to worship God daily is letting creation (and creation's creation) catapult us Godward. There is, however, another method we can use for going Godward: the habit of daily submitting ourselves under the Word of God. This method provides us with spectacles to see the creation-catapult to begin with. What I'm describing is the daily act of reading and meditating on God's word. This is important because "Scripture is the grammar textbook for the language of God, instructing us clearly in the patterns of meaning and the rules by which we are enabled to read everything else."[10] The pagan counterfeit version of this is something like, "Recharging your chi." It's counterfeit because what we're talking about here is not aligning ourselves with *ourselves*; rather, we're conforming ourselves to the revealed will of God.

My great need for this daily habit is quite clear to me personally; I feel all too well the ache in the lyrics of that great hymn "Come Thou Fount of Every Blessing," "Prone to wander, Lord, I feel it! Prone to leave the God I love." The habitual time spent in God's Word is a way for us to cry out, "Here's my heart, Lord, take and seal it. Seal it for thy courts above." I think this is precisely what David was getting at when he wrote, "I rise before the dawn and cry for help; I hope in your words. My eyes are awake before the watches of the night, that I may meditate on your promise." (Ps 119:147–148)

Taking texts like the one just quoted as a cue, I would argue that waking up early and starting the day with a Godward focus is the best way to utilize this method of daily worship. During his earthly ministry, Jesus himself made a point to rise early in the morning to withdraw to a desolate place to pray (Mark 1:35). Not only do we see these wise examples for us in Scripture, but we can also affirm that this time is ideal on practical grounds, can we not? If we are to keep ourselves from being conformed to this world, and instead be transformed by the renewing of our minds, then wouldn't it make sense for us to orient our minds on the transforming word of God *before* facing a world which labors for our conformity?

Of course, it this is by no means without exception, and this kind of communion with God should certainly not be limited to the early morning alone, nor should we make dogmatic statements about what time of day this kind of communion must take place. After all, Jesus also withdrew to a desolate place to pray in the middle of the day (Matt 14:23). Furthermore, Psalm 1 tells us that the man who is blessed is the man who delights in the law of the Lord, and meditates on his law *day and night*, not simply early in the morning (Ps 1:1–2).

A BRIEF WORD ABOUT YOUR BIBLES

The most important thing here is therefore not so much *when* we go Godward in this way, but *that* we go Godward in this way. We must do this. We must come to the Word of God in reverence and humble submission. Not the least reason for this is the fact that God himself has exalted his name and his word above all things (Ps 138:2). While we're on the subject, Psalms have *a lot* of really good things to say about the Word of God. We have already mentioned Psalm 119. You know that psalm; it's the one that boasts 176 verses—the longest chapter in the Bible. And what could such a long Psalm possibly have to say for 176 verses? Basically this: "God, I *love* your Word!"

We should love our bibles.

We should be starving for the Word of God with an eager desire to devour its content. Why? Because God has disclosed himself to us *through his Word!* We don't have to wonder what God is like; he has told us. At least one reason to approach God regularly through his Word, therefore, is that it would be stupid not to. The Creator of the universe has taken time to assure that his attributes, character, and plan for human history would be written down in discernable language, which would be translated into English, printed onto paper, and eventually digitized for user-friendly apps compatible with the smart phone that's probably in your pocket right now. Should we not therefore take advantage of such unprecedented accessibility to the words of life? In David's estimation, the question is not even worth asking. He says, "More to be desired are they than gold, even much fine gold; sweeter also than honey and drippings from the honeycomb" (Ps 19:10). Speaking of this psalm, Charles Spurgeon wrote, "The pleasures arising from a right understanding of the divine testimonies are of the most delightful order; earthly enjoyments are utterly contemptible, if compared with them. The sweetest joys, yea, the sweetest of the sweetest falls to his portion who has God's truth to be his heritage."[11] Put simply, the Word of God is not only the necessary means of knowing the God we should worship, it is also a sweet gift been given by this same God. And one way for us to worship him is to simply enjoy the gifts he has given us.

Characteristics of morning communion

In my experience (which, by God's grace, is continually expanding), this kind of communion will include at least four elements: prayer, reading, meditation, and obedience. Here are some ideas to consider.

Prayer. By default, prayer ought to be a humbling exercise. If we understand prayer properly, we will understand that what's happening is communication between a creature and its Creator. That gives perspective, doesn't it? The one offering prayer finds its origin in dust, which had life breathed into it by the one receiving prayer. The one offering prayer is being sustained by the power of the one receiving prayer. The one offering prayer can only receive, while the one receiving prayer can only give. The one offering prayer is fundamentally needy, while the one receiving prayer is fundamentally in need of nothing whatsoever.

Maintaining this kind of awareness in prayer will necessarily lead to a humble, gospel-centered posture. We will recognize that approaching such transcendent holiness on any merit of our own would be absolutely ludicrous, and we will therefore come boldly to the throne room of God *only* because we know that grace is found there; grace which was purchased by the blood of our Great High Priest. All of this awareness can happen within a split second in prayer.

So what should we pray for during these orienting moments of the day? I usually start simply by thanking God for saving me, for giving me his Word, and for blessing me with the blood-bought privilege of prayer. I then ask for two very basic things; light and heat. This is a simple prayer in which I ask the Spirit of God to give me (1) and understanding of what I'm about to read, and (2) a love for what I'm about to read. So my initial prayer is typically very short, and I allow for spontaneous prayer to occur throughout the rest of my time reading.

Remember, what we're talking about here is an anchor point in the beginning of the day. The idea is to go Godward early in order to orient you in that direction for the rest of the day. You're not being unspiritual if your morning prayer is concise and limited; feel free to let brief flexibility be the mark of this anchor point. This prayer isn't intended to bring you into some high level of spiritual ascendency in preparation for your reading; it's merely a request for God to incline your head and your heart toward the Word you're about to read.

Reading. After the initial prayer is offered, I usually dig right into my reading. There are plenty of daily reading plans to choose from. If you read four chapters a day, you can read through the Bible in a little under a year. The reading plan that I am currently using is one that alternates between the Old Testament and the New Testament, from one of the major biblical genres to another. Some sort of plan that gives you a long-term intake of both Old and New Testaments is preferred because it keeps you from gravitating away from those portions of Scripture you are not naturally inclined toward. This strategy also exposes the reader to the whole corpus of Scripture—with all of its various genres, themes, plots and subplots, all tied together with the grand historical redemptive narrative of Jesus triumphing over Satan, sin, and death.

No matter what type of reading plan you choose, your reading time needs to be guided by some hermeneutical framework. Hermeneutics essentially deals with interpretation; it is the tool we use to determine what a particular text means. Often, all principles of interpretation are thrown out the window during "devotional" reading time. It is the habit of some to read the text in an effort to first answer the question, "What does the text mean *to me*?" rather than the question, "What does this text *mean*?" It is easy for us to forget that the various books of the Bible were written by real people, to real people, in real time and space. This means that questions of genre, intended audience, and historical circumstances are all relevant when reading your Bible.

So, to give some practical examples, this means that Jeremiah 29:11 isn't a promise that you will have a great career, Deuteronomy 28:2 doesn't mean that God has a Lamborghini he intends to drop into your driveway, and Philippians 4:13 has nothing to do with any high school's football team. It also means that David wasn't an idiot for saying that God has placed a tent for the sun in day and in night (Psalm 19:4), and Jesus wasn't an idiot for calling a mustard seed the "smallest seed" (Mark 4:31), just like you wouldn't call me an idiot for commenting on a beautiful "sunset" (rather than a beautiful "earth rotation"), or for saying that *everyone* likes ice cream (when there are certainly some people on this planet—very strange people—who don't like ice cream).

All of this means that part of your devotional reading time may include additional resources to help you answer some of those contextual questions. You may need to get a Bible dictionary to help you understand the historical background of a text. You may need to refer to some commentaries to help you understand a complicated flow of thought. This shouldn't be daunting for you. A common misconception is that studying the Bible seriously and reading the Bible devotionally are two different things. They don't need to be. In fact, they *shouldn't* be.

'Hebrews 4:12–13 does not teach that the *meaning* of Scripture is constantly changing. Some individuals treat the Scripture's "living and active" property as permission to make the text say whatever they want it to say. But the Word of God means what it means. The "living and active" nature of God's word is what makes unchangeable truth *beautiful* in the eyes of a reader. It means that the Holy Spirit who *inspired* the biblical authors to write a text also *illumines* the eyes of the hearts of readers to understand and cherish those texts as he takes those same words and speaks them to the reader.

On the other hand, we should also be careful never to let our hearts drift from our minds when we are reading, and we should also never allow for the fixed nature of the text's meaning to overshadow the intimate and organic nature of God's communication. There most certainly is something mystical happening when the Holy Spirit interacts with us while reading his inspired words, and we ought to consciously read the "Word of God in the presence of God."[12] Something supernatural happens when you read your Bible; you are reading words that *God wrote*. Sure, the Scripture is compiled of letters written by human authors to a human audience in human history, but unlike every other work of human literature, this book has another, more ultimate, Author. At the end of the day, God wrote a book, and he still speaks to people through that same book. So when you read your Bibles, and as you wrestle with the text—following along the argument, striving for the meaning—listen, because God is speaking to you.

There are many other things that could be said about how we should read our Bibles, but one more point that *must* be made is this: we should look for Jesus in every text. This is a hermeneutical principle that should be handled carefully because it could possibly lead the reader into an allegorical imagination land, wherein he does serious harm to the text. I'm not talking about superimposing Jesus into texts that don't have anything to do with him directly and personally; I'm talking about recognizing how a given text contributes to the grand narrative of Scripture, which has Jesus as the hero. His story may not be explicitly in every other story, but every other story is ultimately *in* his story.

Our Lord himself demonstrated this hermeneutical principle when he showed a couple disciples how "Moses, the Prophets," and "all the Scriptures" testified of him, as they strolled down the Emmaus road (Luke 24:27). We see this concept of Christ as the hermeneutical key to the Bible further developed in '2 Corinthians:

> Since we have such a hope, we are very bold, not like Moses, who would put a veil over his face so that the Israelites might not gaze at the outcome of what was being brought to an end. But their minds were hardened. For to this day, when they read the old covenant, that same veil remains unlifted, because only through Christ is it taken away. Yes, to this day whenever Moses is read a veil lies over their hearts. But when one turns to the Lord, the veil is removed. Now the Lord is the Spirit, and where the Spirit of the Lord is, there is freedom. And we all, with unveiled face, beholding the glory of the Lord, are being transformed into the same

> image from one degree of glory to another. For this comes from the Lord who is the Spirit." (2 Cor 3:12–18)

In this passage Paul is explaining how the new covenant, which Jesus ushered in, is indescribably superior to the old covenant, which had been ushered in by Moses. One of his arguments has to do with an understanding of Scripture; whenever "Moses" (referring to the Pentateuch; the first five books of the Bible written by Moses) is read without Jesus, a veil covers the reader's heart. That veil is only removed for the one who turns to Christ. Do you see what Paul is saying? He's saying that you can't understand the Old Testament without Jesus. What a bold statement! Furthermore, Paul is saying that when we view the Bible through this sort of Christocentric lens, we are beholding the glory of the Lord, and it is that vision of God's glory—that is, *Jesus*, portrayed in the Scripture—which transforms us from one degree of glory to another.

Meditation. This word can have a lot of negative connotations, but it shouldn't; it's a Bible word! If our language should be tempered by anything, surely it should be Scripture. So what do I mean by meditation? I don't mean Eastern mystical practices of emptying your mind. Quite the opposite, actually. Biblical meditation isn't the process of thinking less; it's the process of thinking more intensely on one thing—namely, the truth of Scripture.

This means slowly, carefully reading the text, following the thought flow while chewing on your discoveries. It means pausing, reflecting on, and marinating in the truths that grab your attention. This is really the aspect of morning communion with God wherein the reader feeds his soul with the text in an individually tailored way. The important thing is to do this in such a way that you're protecting the integrity of the text. You're not asking, "What does this text mean *to me*?" but rather, "Given that this text means *this*, how should I *feel about that*? How does this timeless truth apply to me today?"

Some days have a more *apparent* bounty of spiritual food than others. Not every time you sit down to read and meditate on Scripture will you find some truth jump out and grip your mind. That's fine. If you're not compelled to worship God because the Scripture is *obviously* nourishing your soul, you can at least be compelled to worship God because the Scripture *is* nourishing your soul—even if it's not apparent to you. It's doing *something*. That prayer might look something like "Lord, I have no idea how that text is shaping my soul. But I thank you for the fact that it *is*. Thank you for using your Word to renew my mind and transform my heart, even when I don't see it working like that."

Obedience. This is the aspect of your morning Bible reading time that sets your trajectory for the rest of the day. Obedience starts with the resolve to obey and is consummated in the act of obedience. The next chapter will primarily deal with what this looks like throughout the rest of your day, so I won't dwell on this issue of obedience here. I'll simply affirm the words of James 1:22–25: if we are hearers of the Word without being doers of the Word, we have tragically deceived ourselves.

I will have failed in my efforts of communication if you walk away from this chapter with the impression that these sequential steps are separated with hardline distinctions—that they only occur one at a time. So keep in mind that the sequential order of prayer, reading, meditation, and obedience is a general outline. There should be some degree of meshing involved as you go through this morning ritual. Your careful attention to prayer, reading, and meditation is, in and of itself, a form of obedience. Likewise, prayer and meditation should be regularly occurring while reading. Furthermore, I offer this method merely as an example; if you feel inclined to accept it as is, I hope it proves fruitful for you. The point is that you should have *some* method of going Godward with devotional Bible reading, and this is one example of what that might look like.

RENEWED TO BE TRANSFORMED

Finally, let's reexamine the purpose of such lengthy details of daily vertical focus. Some may think this chapter is disconnected from the topic of this book. It is not. You cannot direct the people you serve in worship if you are not worshiping. How can you tell them to taste and see that the Lord is good without tasting and seeing his goodness for yourself (Ps 34:1)? However, you do not need to become a super-spiritual, next-level Christian before you can lead people into worship. The biblical instructions we have gleaned from in this chapter are given to *all* Christians. There is no Christian 2.0.

The point is simply that you will serve your people better if you are a habitual worshiper of God. If you come Sunday morning already full with adoration for God, then your worship of God through song will be a burst of doxology that will winsomely compel your fellow brothers and sisters in Christ to join you. So coming to the corporate gathering with eyes that have beheld the glory of God all week is not only something that is necessary for your own soul, but God has also ordained for that holy indulgence of his glory to be a great gift to the believers in your church.

Also, keep in mind, these orienting, Godward moments throughout the day are anchor points. Most of your day is going to be spent focusing on things that aren't God. It must necessarily be this way, for we are finite, and the things of this life will rightfully keep the totality of our attention most of the time. Given that this is an inescapable aspect of being finite, we must understand that these anchor points are necessary for us to navigate through the everyday workings of life in such a way that we are glorifying to God. This is what it means to "discern what is the will of God" (Rom 12:3). If we have our minds regularly renewed with these Godward moments, we will be transformed to worship God as a living sacrifice.

CHAPTER 4

HORIZONTAL DAILY WORSHIP

Part of what it means to worship God daily is to periodically pause to go Godward. In the last chapter I talked about two primary ways we can do that; using creation to catapult us into explicit praise and orienting our days with anchor points of prayer and regular Bible intake. This list can certainly go on. But what about those large portions of the day in between our anchor points of explicit, singularly minded moments of Godwardness? Pauses throughout our day are unique; they don't (and cannot) characterize the bulk of our day. Therefore, we need to have a category of worship that isn't limited to laser-focused adoration for God, or else daily worship would be an impossibility. Thankfully, the Bible does have this kind of category, which we'll call it horizontal daily worship.

THE RIGHT KIND OF WORSHIP WAR

The first stop in our tour of horizontal daily worship expressions is what I like to call the right kind of worship war. You're familiar with the term "worship war" right? It's that classic struggle between the young whippersnappers of the church and the old grey-hairs over what kind of music should characterize the worship service. The young'ns want guitars and drums and—in some severe cases—*electric instruments*. As far as they can tell, florescent lights are the antithesis of a true worship environment, and a line in a song is not truly an expression of worship until the third time it's been sung. In contrast, the older crowd is steadfast in its rejection of projectors and any song that repeats the same line more than twice in a row. They want to sing the good ol' hymns, and they want to sing 'em from the hymnal, dag nabbit! This is the sort of war that often concludes with a split church, either by some members leaving altogether or by starting their own churches within the same building (we call them "traditional" and "contemporary" services).

Of course, I am exaggerating a bit in the above description (though only *a* bit), but the point needs to be made: this kind of worship war is disgraces the church. It dishonors God. However, there *is* a right kind of worship war, a kind that every Christian—and particularly church leaders—should engage daily. I'm talking about a daily war on sin.

Sin is fundamentally a problem of worship. Sin starts with the basic problem of worshiping anything over and against God. This is what it means to "fall short of the glory of God" (Rom 3:23). Paul is not indicting humanity for failing to be as glorious as God; that could never happen. In fact, even if it were *possible* to become as glorious as God, he would never allow it (Isa 48:11). To fall short of the glory of God is to consider God less than glorious; it is to not seek after God (Rom 3:11). In other words, falling short of the glory of God is simply not worshiping him (Rom 1:21). And since, as we have already established, humans *must* worship, to reject God as an object of worship is to worship something else. This is the essence of sin.

So, fundamentally, the war on sin is a war of worship. This is what led one friend to define repentance as "worshiping your way away from fashioned enshrinements to the Rock." Here's the point: worshiping God daily means finding more value in God than in sin. It means you stop looking at porn because porn—though truly and insidiously striking the God-given nerve of sexual desire—is pathetic when compared to the fullness of joy that resides at the right hand of God (Ps 16:11). It means you stop jealousy comparing yourself to other people because your fear of man is eclipsed by your fear of God (Luke 12:4–5). It means you stop trying to fill yourself with the fleeting gratification of money, fame, or power because you realize that they are like drops of muddy water in broken cisterns when compared to God, the fountain of living water and source of all true satisfaction (Jer 2:12–13). So what does it look like to worship God in a world full of temptation? It looks like joyful sin-slaying. That's horizontal worship when sin is in view.

WOR(K)SHIP

Let's get a little more concrete. What about daily worship concerning work? What does that look like? Interestingly enough, the Bible has a thing or two to say about our work ethic. Believe it or not, the biblical standard for our work ethic isn't contingent on our *automatic* enjoyment of what we do. Rather, the biblical command is for us to enjoy *whatever* work God providentially calls us to (Ecclesiastes 3:22; 9:10; 11:5). Enjoyment of your work therefore should not be seen as a prerequisite for choosing a job, it should be seen as obedience to God in whatever job you happen to have! "What are you naturally passionate about?" isn't really the most biblically relevant question when work is in view. In fact, the Bible hardly ever focuses on the particulars of a job but rather the disposition of the heart when that work is done. "*Whatever* you do," Paul says, "work heartily, as for the Lord and not for men" (Col 3:23). There's no caveat here. He doesn't add, "unless you're passionate about something else."

In God's design for the universe, he has given us certain avenues to take for our worship of him, and one of those avenues is work. It is an expression of our love for God; he is pleased by our efforts to work hard and do well in our jobs to his glory.

In their helpful and practical book, *The Gospel At Work: How Working for King Jesus Gives Purpose and Meaning to Our Jobs*, Sebastian Traeger and Greg Gilbert illustrate this concept poignantly: "Your love for God should motivate you to work, no matter the particulars of what you do, 'with your whole heart.' If you are a mother, work at it with all your heart, as working for the Lord. If you are a student, work at it with all your heart, as working for the Lord. If you make cars, close sales, litigate, or medicate, do it as if you were working for the Lord himself—because you are! You love God; therefore work with all your heart!"[13]

Our jobs were never supposed to be a punishment, nor were they ever designed to be an unfortunate necessity. Work isn't a defect; it's a feature. The concept of vocation predates the fall; we see work all the way back in the garden of Eden, when Adam is commanded to work it and subdue it (Gen 1:28). In fact, the Hebrew word translated as "work" in this passage is the same word translated as "service" in temple worship-service. Adam and Eve were commanded by God to *serve* (just like how temple priests were commanded to *serve* in temple worship) in the garden. Work unto God is worship of God. This truth actually gives us some concrete connections between our contributions in work and the glory of God in this world.

Speaking of Genesis 1:28, Joe Rigney writes: "The call to subdue the earth means that the earth, as originally given to man, was unsubdued, undomesticated. This implies that creation has unrealized potential, latent dimensions that lie beneath the surface...Culture, then, is a kind of cultivation, a drawing out what God has put in. Or, to change metaphors, culture is an adornment of creation, the further beautification of an already beautiful world. . . . In a word, Creation + Man's Creative Efforts = Culture."[14]

Do you see what he's saying here? Our work is pleasing to God not only because it is itself an expression of worship, but also because it contributes to the shaping of God's creation! That God's intention was always to have a world cultivated by man puts a whole new spin on our work. This is at least part of what it means to be made in the image of God; we have been profoundly blessed with the privilege of imitating him in our work. This is true of every legitimate vocation.[15]

Hear me, music leader, your position in your local church is not the only possible work you can do to the glory of God. If you work as a barista, work hard to give your customer a well-crafted drink; this pleases the Lord. If you're a banker, work hard for the success of your employer and for your customer's peace of mind; this pleases the Lord. If you are a plumber, work hard to bless your clients with dependable plumbing; this pleases the Lord. If you are a student, work hard to excel in your studies; this pleases the Lord. If you are a mother, work hard to raise and nurture your children for their temporal and eternal good (even when your hard work goes unrecognized); this pleases the Lord.

YOUR WORK HAS AN ESCHATOLOGY

All of this means that, for the Christian who works as unto the Lord, nothing is wasted. Nothing is meaningless. No email you send is insignificant. No software code you tweak is without purpose. All of your work is contributing to an uncultivated world that God intends to cultivate through your seemingly minute and mundane activities.

And, contrary to popular belief, the fall has not reversed this reality. The common conception for many Christians is that we're all on this sinking ship, waiting for it to go under, and any effort to keep the thing afloat is a complete waste of time. But this is a misconception. Of course we should walk around with a real awareness that this current world is not our home; we are sojourners in search of our native, heavenly homeland. Things on this planet are not as they should be. But the glorious hope of the resurrection is that things on this *planet will become* as they should be! This is what creation groans for (Rom 8:19–22, 2 Cor 5:4–5). And however you believe this whole end-of-the-age thing is going down, one thing is certain: Jesus is going to turn every tragedy on its head. Mortality will be swallowed up by immortality. Every one step backward will be transformed into two steps forward.

The final product isn't going to be some strange, ethereal floaty place, populated by little fat babies playing on golden harps. We're not looking to be unclothed—we're not looking forward to a bodiless existence—we're anticipating a resurrection! We're anticipating Eden 2.0; a thick, redeemed, glorified universe where food tastes better, and color is more vibrant, and music is lovelier. We're looking forward to a world that makes this fallen, groaning one look like a ghostly, transparent, grey city.[16]

We know this is what look forward to because King Jesus has promised to make all things new (Rev 21:5). Furthermore, God has proven he is equal to the task; he knows how to make wickedness an agent of good (Gen 50:20); he knows how to make folly an agent of wisdom (1 Cor 1:21); he knows how to make weakness an agent of strength (2 Cor 12:10); he knows how to make affliction an agent of glory (2 Cor 4:17); and he knows how to make death an agent of life (1 Cor 15:42–45). In all of this we can rest assured that Jesus is able to redeem the monotonous work you do. Your work has an eschatology.

WORSHIP THROUGH FISH TACOS

Let's go a step further. What about horizontal worship where simple things like food and laughter and TV and road trips and novels and naps are concerned? In the last chapter I shared a story in which a Utah sunset launched me into explicitly Godward worship. Certainly my singing of "How Great Thou Art" was expressed my worship, but so is enjoying the scene that preceded it. Think of it like this: If you are in an art gallery and want to honor a great painter, one way to do this is by telling him that you admire him as an artist. Another way, however, is simply by admiring his artwork.

Or imagine a young boy on Christmas morning. How does a little boy honor his parents for buying him a much-wanted toy? He can say, "Thank you." But after that he continues to honor them by smiling from ear to ear and enjoying the toy. His eyes are no longer fixed explicitly on his parents, but he is still honoring them. His glad reception of the good honors his parents. To be sure, it is possible for the boy to receive the gift in such a way that he forgets about the giver; there is a way for him to show ingratitude and thus idolize the gift—to consider the gift to be more important than the giver. But that such an attitude is *possible* should not then lead the boy to abandon every gift his parents have graciously given him; they *want* to see him enjoy what their gifts!

This is important because we are finite; we cannot do everything at once. We cannot go explicitly and singularly Godward while simultaneously giving our full attention to the various things we are told to attend to. There are many aspects of our nature that can be chalked up to the fall, but our finitude is not one of them.

Joe Rigney is helpful in understanding this: "Our existence in time, space, and bodies is not a bug; it's a feature, designed by infinite wisdom for the communication of the unfathomable riches of his glory. God is not frustrated by our finitude. He is not hamstrung by our bodies. Our limitations pose no barrier to him. 'He knows our frame; he remembers that we are dust' (Ps. 103:14). *He made us this way*, and he thinks it was a grand idea."[17]

Do you see what he's saying? You shouldn't feel guilty about focusing exclusively on that which is right before you. You shouldn't feel guilty about playing with your kids and getting entirely lost in the music of their laughter. You shouldn't feel guilty about spending your absolute attention on the exam you're studying for. You shouldn't feel guilty about enjoying a night out with your friends doing non-Bible-study activities. You shouldn't feel guilty about having sex with your wife and not praying at the same time.

This is important to understand if we want to affirm that the Bible is consistent. For example, Paul isn't setting us up for failure when he says, "Set your mind on things that are above, not on things that are on earth" (Col 3:2), and then follows that imperative up with a bunch of instructions about how to think about the things of earth (Col 3:12–25). Paul doesn't contradict himself in this. Again, Rigney: "A mind that is set on the things above spends an awful lot of time thinking about things on the earth. Family, neighbors, church, job, earthly responsibilities—the person governed by heavenly things intentionally and deliberately considers and engages them. The heavenly mindset is profoundly earthy, but it is fundamentally oriented by the glory of Christ."[18]

Think about the first recorded words spoken by man in the Bible. God had just declared that Adam's solitude was not good, and he met Adam's need with a wife. As soon as Adam gazed on his beautiful wife, he broke out into song. "This at last! Bone of my bones and flesh of my flesh!" (Gen 2:18–25) Who was the object of Adam's song? Not God. Was this sinful? Absolutely not! This glorious scene predates the fall.[19] Adam is honoring an Artist by praising his artwork. He is a child honoring his parents by ecstatically enjoying his present. He is a worshiper worshiping God by enjoying his gift!

Again, Rigney sums this point up potently: "What does full and supreme love for God look like when it meets one of his gifts? Glad reception and enjoyment of his gifts. Delight in Eve is what full and supreme love for God looks like when it meets Eve. Grateful enjoyment of fish tacos is what supreme love for God looks like when it eats fish tacos. Robust pleasure in church softball is what supreme love for God looks like when it plays church softball. Delight in people and love for people is what supreme and full love for God looks like when it meets people."[20]

I have saved this aspect of daily worship for last because it is largely involuntary and needs to be calibrated by other forms of daily worship. No one needs to be told to enjoy the things of this earth. That comes very naturally. Your unbelieving neighbor doesn't need to be taught how to enjoy fish tacos as his source of delight; he knows how to do that. He *doesn't* know how to enjoy them as a gift; he doesn't know how to treat them as aids in worshiping God. Therefore, it is important that we first establish what kind of universe we exist in—the kind that has a Lord. We need to train ourselves to see the thread that ties every gift back to the hand of its Giver.[21] Then, between those moments of orientation, we should conform to the biblical trajectory *in* this universe. Worship God by thanking him for fish tacos. Then, worship God by enjoying fish tacos.

TRAILBLAZERS OF WORSHIP

So what does all of this have to do with leading corporate worship? Remember, your responsibility as a music leader is to invite your congregation to do what you are doing. A musical-worship leader who is worshiping God daily is inviting his congregation to a daily lifestyle of worship. As a musical-worship leader, you should be a trailblazer of daily worship. Daily worship should characterize your life in all of its manifestations: orienting anchor points of exclusive Godwardness, passionate and worshipful sin-slaying, and robust, doxological enjoyment of God's many gifts. This is how you consistently worship God in spirit and truth. This is how you are a *daily* worshiper of God rather than a Sunday-morning performer. The overflow of such a life culminating on Sunday morning will serve your people in ways you can't even dream of.

CHAPTER 5
BROKEN & BUILT

For the first two years of our marriage, my wife I lived in a little house just south of Kansas City. I worked at UPS and Starbucks as I finished up my undergraduate degree while my wife began her career as an elementary school teacher. During that time we were very involved in a nearby church pastored by my father-in-law. In the course of those two years I served in various capacities, from teaching a Sunday School class, to serving as an interim Youth Pastor, to regularly leading worship through song. We left that church after I accepted a part-time position as a music leader in a nearby church plant, where I served for about six months. Neither of these churches were healthy by any stretch of the imagination, and by the time we moved on campus at seminary, my wife and I were both spiritually exhausted.

To be sure, this season was beneficial, and it has proven to be a sanctifying part of our life. But it was life-draining. The former church was plagued with the controlling influence of a deacon who was likely unregenerate (to name just one of its issues), and the latter was an aspiring attractional church, which was about as theologically shallow as the yellow-tinted section of the public pool. No church is perfect, and frustrations will abound everywhere, but this season was uniquely tiring. However, the difficulty of this season cannot be reduced to manipulative deacons or a vain pastor; what made this season so intolerable was spiritual loneliness.

We were completely without spiritual kinsmen in either of these churches—there were a few likeminded brothers and sisters in these ministry contexts, and they were like oxygen to us. Every conversation that was even the slightest bit theologically enriching (which, admittedly, always occur too seldom for the theology student) was like a brief moment of resurfacing from the drowning status quo. But having a couple of likeminded brothers and sisters to have the occasional "spiritual" conversation with is no remedy for spiritual loneliness. This kind of loneliness is something that can only be dealt with through gospel-saturated community—the kind of community that is meaty with enough theology to strengthen your resolve yet which also leaves in the fat and gristle and bone of grace and imperfections and confrontations of sin.

A BIBLICAL PATTERN

So far we haven't dealt with concepts that are uniquely applicable to music leaders—we have been talking about worship conceptually, which makes our discussion thus far universally applicable to all Christians everywhere. This chapter is no exception. We now turn our attention to a clear biblical pattern of the Christian life: being broken and being built.

Acts 4 presents a perfect case study for this pattern. This episode comes on the heels of two famous evangelistic discourses by Peter. The first was in chapter 3, when he preached to the gawking crowds after God healed the lame beggar with those immortal words, "I have no silver and gold, but what I do have I give to you. In the name of Jesus Christ of Nazareth, rise up and walk!" (Acts 3:6). The second discourse occurred the following day when Peter doubled down in his Christ-exalting resolve to his accusers, who had imprisoned him for preaching the gospel. Immediately following their release, Peter and John came back to their friends to fill them in on what had just taken place:

> When they were released, they went to their friends and reported what the chief priests and the elders had said to them. And when they heard it, they lifted their voices together to God and said, "'Sovereign Lord, who made heaven and the earth and the sea and everything in them, who through the mouth of our father David, your servant, said by the Holy Spirit, 'Why did the Gentiles rage, and the peoples plot in vain? The kings of the earth set themselves, and the rulers were gathered together, against the Lord and against his Anointed'— for truly in this city there were gathered together against your holy servant Jesus, whom you anointed, both Herod and Pontius Pilate, along with the Gentiles and the peoples of Israel, to do whatever your hand and your plan had predestined to take place. And now, Lord, look upon their threats and grant to your servants to continue to speak your word with all boldness, while you stretch out your hand to heal, and signs and wonders are performed through the name of your holy servant Jesus.'" (Acts 4:23–30)

Don't miss the dynamic. We can summarize the entire episode in five movements. (1) Peter and John faithfully and boldly proclaim the gospel (Acts 3:11–26). (2) Peter and John are confronted and persecuted for their faithful proclamation (Acts 4:1–7). (3) Peter defends the faith against opposition (Acts 4:8–22). (4) Peter and John regroup with their fellow brothers and sisters

(Acts 4:23). (5) These brothers and sisters pray for Peter and John, that they would have boldness to go back out and start the process all over again.

This scene, and many others in the New Testament, communicates a pattern central to the Christian life: the Christian is broken, and the Christian is built up. You go out into the world and preach the gospel, only to get chewed up and spit back out into your community of saints, who will encourage you and challenge you to go back out into the world to preach the gospel. This dynamic is a recipe for tension; if we are living out this reality, there is a sense in which we are always burdened with a sort of holy discontentment.

The world drenches us with one soul-jolting bucket of depravity after another, and we become discontented with the suicidal idolatry that surrounds us. We are thus driven into our churches, where we can worship the true and living God in a spiritually "naked and unashamed" kind of way—a way in which we can simply revel in, rather than argue for, the gospel. But as we do this another kind of holy discontentment bubbles up, a kind that finds lostness intolerable, a that forces us to look at that suicidal idolatry with a renewed evangelistic pity. We see how pathetic the world's object of worship is in relation to our own, and we are compelled to offer them something (*Someone*) better! And when we do, the resistance and abiding depravity that meets us drives us back into our churches to start the process all over again.

WORSHIP AMONG PAGANS

At the center of this dynamic, as you might have guessed, is worship. On the one hand, we worship among pagans, and on the other hand, we worship alongside saints. I want to first briefly examine the former. Christians are broken and emptied when they worship among pagans in a couple of ways.

One is simply by looking at pagan worship for what it is. Let's take two examples of worldly worship: sexual licentiousness and child sacrifice.

PAGAN WORSHIP: SEXUAL LICENTIOUSNESS

In June 2015 the *Huffington Post* published an article entitled, "These 21 Words About Sex May Be the Most Important Words Miley Cyrus Has Ever Said." What, you may be asking, are these 21, paradigm-shifting, revolutionary words? Read "em and weep (literally): "I am literally open to every single thing that is consenting and doesn't involve an animal and everyone is of age." No, I didn't make this article up. These are the *groundbreaking*, "most important 21 words about sex" from the cannon-ball-riding prophetess of the sexual revolution.

In this article, the author pinpoints what he assumes to be the problem plaguing our society: "Until we realize that the way we have systematically designed our relationships and families has been and continues to be flawed, we're going to be stuck making the same mistakes and saddled with the same problems, from cheating and divorce to unwanted pregnancies and sexually transmitted infections to depression and anxiety."[22]

Note: a non-negotiable in every worldview is the assumption that something is fundamentally wrong with the world, that we all are in serious trouble and are in need of help is an indisputable fact. And every worldview offers a "gospel" as the solution to whatever problem it identifies. For example, communism says that the problem with the world is individuality and lack of uniformity—the gospel according to communism is essentially the eradication of individuality by a superimposing and micromanaging totalitarian government. Buddhism says that the problem with the world is suffering brought about by desire—the gospel according to Buddhism is the eradication of desire through sheer discipline. The sexual revolution represented in the quote above insists that the problem with the world is sexual boundaries. What is the cause of adultery, divorce, unwanted pregnancies, STDs and even depression? Self-control! So what is their "gospel?" Let's let them speak for themselves: "The point is that our desires, whatever they may be, shouldn't be ignored or left untended to rot or they'll be our downfall. Sex is not the enemy, it's the answer. So let's start getting dirty so we can join Miley in cleaning up our sex-shaming culture."[23]

The gospel according to the sexual revolution is indulgence. Liberation through unbridled, untamed indulgence of our fleshly desires. This is the liberty they offer: we will rid ourselves of adultery and divorce and unwanted pregnancies and STDs and, yes, even depression by throwing out all sexual rule books and diving headfirst into whatever feels good.

Let that just sink in for a minute.

Having a hard time with safeguarding the fidelity of your marriage? Just recapitulate adultery as "liberated sexual expression"; you can't break the rules if there are none! Tired of your depression? Just go out and get laid; that's the answer to all your sorrows! Afraid of STDs? Just go crazy and . . . oh wait . . . how is this one supposed to work again?

I don't think I need to explain that this is all madness. This message rightly exacerbates Christians. It makes us angry. The apostles of this movement are leading the masses into self-destruction—personally, sociologically, and eternally. It makes us sorrowful. The number of victims left in the wake of this high treason against God is growing, and it breaks our heart to see it. But it also makes us tired and thirsty. It is draining to be surrounded by such insanity, and we need to hear some saintly voices of reason to interrupt the white noise of babbling worldliness. Watching thirsty worshipers shovel buckets of sand down their throats whets our whistles for the Fountain of living water!

PAGAN WORSHIP: CHILD SACRIFICE

In July 2015 an organization called The Center for Medical Progress released the first of a series of videos taken from an undercover investigative journalism project.[24] David Daleiden initiated the project to expose Planned Parenthood and their affiliates for their illegal activities of buying and selling aborted fetuses. These videos cover everything from interviews with leading Planned Parenthood officials to tours of Planned Parenthood facilities and the footage of dismembered babies. They are, without a doubt, some of the most gruesome, gut-wrenching videos ever to reach such wide exposure online.

Just to name a few of the horrors documented in these videos:

- They show a Planned Parenthood executive describing, in thorough detail, how abortionists will change their standard procedures and use ultrasound technology in order to hack up unborn babies with enough precision to preserve their highly marketable limbs. She describes these processes all while eating a salad and drinking wine.
- They show an executive haggling over prices for baby body parts, eventually divulging her motivation: "I want a Lamborghini!"
- They show a woman laughing at the imaginary scenario of opening a package to find a baby's severed head staring back at her.
- They show the image of tweezers sifting through a petri dish of body parts with the background voice of an abortion doctor, gleefully exclaiming, "It's a boy!"
- They show the image of an aborted baby *dying* on another petri dish, slowly moving his foot.

I could go on and on. As you can imagine, these videos picked up quite a bit of attention for a time. There was a time in which everyone knew what you meant when you described "the videos."

And then they were forgotten.

As if they had never happened.

Just like that, and Planned Parenthood went back slicing and dicing. Business as usual. These videos may have been unsettling to the society in which they were released, but they weren't paradigm shifting for this very simple reason: *there was little they exposed*.

Don't misunderstand me, these videos brought about many new revelations. But what they *exposed* was the horror of abortion, which has always been horrendous. These videos shined a spotlight on barbaric people doing (big surprise) barbaric acts. The shocking thing about this whole revelation is how shocking it was to Christians and how unshocking it was to the world. The people of our society didn't collectively pause and shriek in horror, "What have we done?!" There was no mass repentance or revival. Instead, our society doubled-down in its celebration of abortion, even coming up with a social media hashtag that knocked the wind out of many of us: #shoutyourabortion.

But should we have been surprised by any of this? What invisible line was crossed to make these acts so intolerable? Would it somehow be *less* barbaric if these hitmen used ultrasound technology to dismember little babies and then threw the remains into the dumpster rather than selling them for a profit? Let's be real here, Planned Parenthood didn't get more evil when it decided to get even more bang for its buck by getting into the business of body snatching; it has always been a human slaughterhouse, which is about as vile as you can get.

Why do I mention all of this? Simply to illustrate this truth: our culture is pagan; it engages in pagan worship. It may sound extreme to call abortion "sacrificial worship," but think about it. The object of desire behind every abortion is self. "I don't want to have a child. I am not ready to bring a child into this world. I still have so much 'life ahead of me.'" A pregnant self-worshiper can only continue in her pious devotion to herself if she sacrifices her baby. An inseminating self-worshiper can only continue in his pious devotion to himself if he sacrifices his baby (either through abandonment or pressure to have him or her executed). Raising a child requires a level of self-sacrifice that many in our society object to because *it's against their religion.*

So self-worshipers come to the designated temples erected for the praise of self (abortion clinics), and they offer their children to the priests of self (abortion doctors), who fulfill their priestly duties (baby-hacking) in their priestly garments (lab coats and medical gloves). I don't believe I could imagine a more fitting modern recapitulation of Moloch worship if I tried. So what's the Christian response to all of this? Again, it is anger, sadness, resolve, and protest, but it is also exhaustion. It breaks us and drives us back into community with other believers. As Christians, being surrounded by houses of Moloch awakens our desire to be in the house of Yahweh.

PAGAN RESISTANCE

Another way Christians are broken when they spend time in the world is when the world breaks them. Christians are behind enemy lines when they venture into the world to worship among pagans, and to expect to receive anything less than full-fledged resistance is just plain foolish. You have to read the New Testament with your eyes closed to miss the central theme of suffering in the Christian life.[25] This really does make sense when we stop to consider what becoming Christ-like actually is. Becoming like Christ is becoming like the "man of sorrows," the suffering servant who was murdered at the hands of lawless men. We most resemble Jesus when we suffer.

Being rejected and mocked and beaten down for our faith is to be expected because our message is fundamentally offensive and stupid to the natural person. No one in their right mind will take the gospel seriously unless the Holy Spirit opens their eyes to see its truth. Let's just go over the bullet points to remind us of what we *actually* believe.

In believing the gospel, we Christians believe:

- A virgin conceived and gave birth to the God-man.
- All of heaven came to announce the most important event in human history (the incarnation) to men from one of the most despised classes in society (shepherds).
- Heaven designated the most obscure and insignificant people to serve as hype-men for the Messiah.
- God the Son chose country bumpkins and mobsters and hookers to be his followers during his earthly ministry.
- He defeated Satan, sin, and death by dying on a cross like a common criminal (he's a conqueror who conquered by being conquered).
- He was raised from the dead three days later (go ahead and say that one out loud if you need to).
- And after that, he ate some fish, walked through walls, and floated up into heaven. Also, he's going to come back riding on a white horse with a massive tattoo on his thigh and a flaming sword sticking out of his mouth, and he's going to right every wrong and wipe away every tear when he sets up his kingdom that will last forever and ever.

. . . that is what we believe . . .

That is *simply foolish* to the natural person! And no amount of sophisticated and flowery language can hide the fact that our gospel is a stench to nostrils that have not been divinely conditioned to find it a sweet fragrance. By the way, this means that we actually shouldn't be afraid when we evangelize! When you're questioning, "Is this person going to think I sound stupid?" Don't worry, you don't have to wonder: they definitely will think you're stupid! *Unless* God chooses to open the eyes of their hearts to see how beautiful the gospel actually is. "For we are the aroma of Christ to God among those who are being saved and among those who are perishing, to one a fragrance from death to death, to the other a fragrance from life to life" (2 Cor 2:15–16).

The gospel is only sweet or sickening; it's only beautiful or ugly—and whether it's received one way or another does not rest on your shoulders or your ability to speak eloquently. That depends on the sovereign will of God, who will either take your words and use them to penetrate the hearts of your listeners so they see the beauty of the gospel, or he won't. In which case your listeners will mock you at best, or kill you at worst—which will either bring about your sanctification or your glorification. That's what we call a classic win-win situation. But I digress.

All this to say, worship—yes, *worship*—confronts. Our scent is a stench in the nostrils of nonbelievers and our shouts of praise are like nails on a chalkboard to them. If Christians are being consistently Christian out in the world, they will get beaten up and driven back into the community of other Christians. But the converse is also true: if Christians are being consistently Christian in their community of other believers, they will be built up and driven back into the world.

WORSHIP ALONGSIDE SAINTS

There is a danger in only living out one half of this broken-built dynamic, which is precisely what left me exhausted during the season I described at the beginning of this chapter. I was heartbroken and exacerbated by the pagan worship around me. I was also regularly confronted about my faith in my work contexts, and because of this I was constantly in a defensive disposition—my boxing gloves were always on. But I was left without the life-giving experience of simple Christian community. Don't get me wrong, evangelism and apologetics *are* life-giving endeavors in and of themselves, and they are unique expressions of worship. However, this is only half the dynamic that God intends for his people to live in. When your every "Jesus Christ is Lord!" is met with "No he's not!" you eventually yearn to simply hear "Amen!" And when you finally *do* get your "Amen," it's like manna from heaven!

In addition to worship in the corporate gathering,[26] another crucial way Christians are built up is for them to live out meaningful relationships with one another in a more intimate setting. Of course, one implies the other. Remember, one of the ways we "teach and admonish" one another in corporate worship is when we ascribe worth to God in the midst of—and because of—the trials we are currently facing, which *necessitates* genuine community outside of the corporate gathering (how can my brothers and sisters learn by seeing me worship in the midst of my trials if they don't know that I'm in the midst of trials?).

So what should this kind of life-on-life engagement look like? It at least looks intentional. If you're waiting to stumble upon this kind of community accidentally, it will never happen—at least, not in the kind of society we find ourselves in. You will have to actually pencil this in. If you're not currently serving in a church context where this sort of thing is encouraged and facilitated, you may have to take the initiative to start a Bible study or prayer group on your own. I have been forced to do this in the past. During those spiritually lonely years of ministry, my wife and I began a Tuesday night Bible study with every like-minded Christian we could think of—some were church members, some were not.

In all honesty, I don't think that I was equipped to lead such a group, and it was mostly a disaster, but we nevertheless puttered along, swimming against the grain to do something that none of us were conditioned to do by our respective churches. This is not ideal, and if there is any possible way to live in community within the context of your local church—under the authority of your own pastors—you need to do that. But if Christian community is like oxygen for the believer (and it is), you need to do whatever you can to keep from suffocating.

I repeat, music leader: *you must be involved in Christian community*. It's not an option. It's not a supplement. It's *infinitely* more important than your song choice, your ability to sing, or your service as a music leader. Your church doesn't need a music leader who is going about the Christian life autonomously; such a person will wreak havoc on the body.

So what does a healthy community group look like? We shouldn't get dogmatic about what specifically happens during these meetings. For example, should the group be a Bible study, a book study, or discussion group covering the content of sermons? Should the men and women split up at any point during the group? How long should the group meet? Should the group ever break from its regular routine to simply have a meal or game night? There is flexibility in all of this.

The main point is that there is some kind of avenue for you and your fellow brothers and sisters to be knit together in love. What you want to see developed over time is something we refer to at my church as *gospel fluency*: the ability to view all of life through the lens of what God has done in Christ. You want to develop an instinct to both *reflect* the gospel in your actions toward one another and to *remind* each other of the gospel by consistently pointing each other to Christ.

This shouldn't be superficial or mechanical. Reflecting the love of God in Christ may simply look like weeping with those who weep, or it may look like confronting sinful attitudes that are not in step with the gospel, or it may look like throwing up your hands and praying about a seemingly unresolvable issue, or it may look like reaching down into your pockets to pay for the groceries of a struggling brother or sister. Keep in mind, this lifestyle is counterintuitive to the residents of an individualistic, self-serving society. What we are talking about is a fundamental shift, from having a default self-centered disposition to having a default others-centered disposition. It's hard work to foster an environment for people that is altogether unlike every other environment to which they are accustomed. This means that it must be wrought by the Holy Spirit and navigated intentionally. Let me humbly offer a few suggestions for what you can do to contribute to this sort of thing.

Set ground rules. Certain sinful tendencies often creep in to disrupt this kind of healthy community, so naming them and banishing them from the beginning can be very helpful. In our church, there are three rules for our community group discussions. The first rule is that group members must speak for themselves, staying away from deflecting "we" language. Often people speak in generalities to avoid naming personal sins or needs. This can serve as a defense mechanism, and you want that removed; the closer you can get to being spiritually naked and unashamed, the better.

Our second rule is that community group members must not "rescue" one another. What we mean by "rescuing" one another is jumping the gun to offer "fixes" for expressed problems, or seeking to cut through the tension in a room by cracking a joke. This sort of thing is difficult to quantify, but you know it when you see it: a guy is sharing some deep insecurities and is on the verge of tears, the entire room is filled with thick tension, and then suddenly someone breaks the silence with a lighthearted observation or joke and the tension dissolves into collective chuckles. Meanwhile, the guy who was formerly on the brink of actually bearing his heart for his community group shrinks back into isolation. We should strive to keep that from happening. It's a product of insecurity and fear of vulnerability, and it disrupts healthy dialogue.

The third rule is that *community group members must not engage in "sidebar" conversations*. This can be with other members in the group or on smart phones. There are few things more discouraging in a community group setting than sharing a prayer request or confessing sins to a room full of people who are preoccupied with their phones or with conversations with one another, not to mention what such a behavior communicates to the most insecure introvert who already doubts that he or she has anything valuable to offer the group. This sort of thing is a community killer that should be forbidden in a healthy community group.

Prayer. This one is obvious, but it is nevertheless *crucial*. One of the primary ways we share one another's burdens is by collectively lifting them up and laying them before the feet of Jesus. Sometimes the best response to our great Shepherd's invitation, "Come to me, all you who are weary and heavy laden, and I will give you rest," is for *less* weary brother and sisters to carry the weariest from among their midst to Jesus themselves (being fully prepared to lower them down through the housetop roof if they have to). Prayer is one of the most effective ways to knit Christians together in love, not only in the act of praying *for* one another but in the act of praying *with* one another. Collectively coming to the same God with the same need or request or praise or complaint is a binding experience.

Confession. This is another one that ought to be obvious, but I fear it isn't. Growing in Christ-likeness is a communal endeavor that includes (though is not limited to) sin slaying. Make no mistake, you need others in your fight against sin. I don't use that word "need" lightly; I genuinely do believe that it is *impossible* for sin to be laid to rest unless it is confessed. This is particularly true of secret sins committed in the dark—sins that aren't apparent to those around you. An obvious example of this would be the sin of lust in general and the indulgence of pornography in particular. I speak from experience when I say that confession (to others, not just private confession to God) is necessary for putting habitual indulgence of pornography to death.

So let me make this very clear—and yes, I will be dogmatic about *this*—if you are currently in the throes of this strangling sinful habit, *you have to confess it*. If you are married, *you have to confess it to your spouse*. Do it today. Put the book down and plan this confession out. Confess to a friend first if you need to (someone who won't let you get away with backing out of confession to your spouse). Failure to do so is nothing less than deception, and you know this. If you are not married, *you have to confess it to someone.*

This, by the way, is why general confession in a community group setting can be so fruitful. It is extremely difficult because in so doing you are becoming incredibly vulnerable; the greater the number of people who know about your sin, the greater the potential of seeing that information abused. However, multiplying the number of hearers in your confession also multiplies the number of soldiers to help you fight against sin; it results in a united front and a large reservoir of accountability.

Be cautious, however—specifically when it comes to sexual sin—with how and what you confess in an open, mixed-gender setting. What I'm laying out here is a principle of corporate intercession: the more intercessors you have fighting on your behalf the better. But applying this principle requires wisdom; it may be wise for many (most, even) for some sexual sins to be confessed in same-gender groups and others in mixed-gender groups. Regardless, you *should be confessing your sins to others.*

This sort of thing does not come naturally. Effort is required to foster the kind of environment that engenders confession. One way to do this is to meet genuine confession and repentance with immediate grace. There is something truly potent about naming a sin and then hearing another Christian speak on behalf of God to say, "*That* sin—the sin that causes you to experience such shame and condemnation—has been *nailed to the cross*. You no longer bear it! In Christ the Father sees you as clean as Jesus. That sin is not your master, and we—as your brothers and sisters—will covenant to see to it that it is placed under your grace-empowered boot heal *where it belongs*."

RESIDENT ALIENS AND ELECT EXILES—BROKEN & BUILT AS IDENTITY

Take these concrete suggestions (or leave them) for what they're worth. They are suggestions, after all. In all honesty, most of these things are simply godly intuition. Christians *want* to share the gospel with the lost; to the degree that they don't, they are being inconsistent with their Christianity. And Christians *want* to spend time with other Christians; to the degree that they don't, they are being inconsistent with their Christianity. If you are being faithful, you aren't likely content having one without the other for long. On the one hand, if you could spend your entire life in Christian community without feeling compelled in any way to go out into the world with the gospel, your Christian community is defective. Something isn't working properly. On the other hand, if you could spend your entire life in a sinful world without having an aching and yearning desire to commune with other Christians, your witness is defective and you have likely gone to bed with worldliness.

Fundamentally, this discontentedness is the Christian's identity. Peter refers to Christians as "elect exiles" (1 Pet 1:1) Don't miss the striking nature of that title! Christians are "elect"—they are chosen, beloved, cherished by God, citizens of heaven; and they are "exiles"—they are rejected, despised, outcasts, homeless sojourners on earth. Christians, in other words, are oxymorons.

God has called us to experience both "at-homeness" (with God and with one another) and "homesickness" while we are on this earth. This is why Peter can say, with one breath, "But you are a chosen race, a royal priesthood, a holy nation, a people for his own possession, that you may proclaim the excellencies of him who called you out of darkness into his marvelous light," and then in the next say, "Beloved, I urge you *as sojourners and exiles* to abstain from the passions of the flesh, which wage war against your soul. Keep your conduct among the gentiles honorable, so that when they speak against you as evildoers, they may see your good deeds and glorify God on the day of visitation" (1 Pet 2:9–12)

This is why, music leader, the corporate gathering is so crucial. If you are not living in this already/not yet tension, you will lose the gravity of what it means for your brothers and sisters to come together as one body. When Christians gather together, they are getting a taste of heaven—as foreigners in another country, they are stepping foot onto an embassy of their heavenly homeland where they belong. They are experiencing, in a real sense, what they have to look forward to for eternity! However, on account of the fact that these gatherings are *unique*, Christians are reminded that all is not as it will be. Where heaven will consist of perpetual fellowship and worship, here on earth their every time together is marked by a start time and an end time. Where heaven will consist of the great feast of the Lamb, with Christ Jesus and all of his elect, here on earth their corporate meal consists of two very basic elements: bread and wine. Thus, the broken and built life is nothing short of the Christian life, and our gatherings are potent reminders of our calling to be both broken *and* built until glory—they are opportunities to simultaneously pray, "Thank you, Lord Jesus, for coming!" and "Come quickly, Lord Jesus!"

CHAPTER 6
DISSECTING THE PLATFORM

At long last we have arrived at the portion of the book that may or may not be what you, gracious reader, were looking for when you first picked up this little volume. Everything we have explored thus far in the book has been big-picture stuff—I've tried to make clear what Christian worship is, and thus, while the preceding material may be especially important for Christians who serve the body by leading worship through song, it applies directly to any Christian, regardless of vocation. This chapter marks a major shift, however: for these next two chapters everything else I have to say is uniquely crucial for music leaders and pastors.

WHAT IS A "WORSHIP LEADER"?

We must begin with the awkward admission that the position we see in virtually every evangelical church today entitled "worship leader" is foreign to the New Testament. The situation is actually a lot worse than you might expect; it's not merely that the term "worship leader" isn't found in the pages of Scripture (that's not really a big deal—"*Trinity*" isn't a term we get from Scripture directly either), it's that the New Testament doesn't even describe *the role*. Yet, it is so common in most churches that one would expect for it to be an office of the church, sharing its own list of qualifications alongside elders and deacons in Titus and 1 Timothy: "And likewise, *the worship dude* must be the husband of one wife, able to play at least four chords on the guitar, and he must be willing to ramble about what's on his heart. He must not take theology too seriously, and he must commit to repeat the bridge of every song no less than four times."[27] Unfortunately for many worship dudes, that's not in the Bible.

Bob Kauflin summarizes the situation:

> So how important are worship leaders? And what should they actually be doing? These questions aren't as easy to answer as we might think. First, it's hard to find a clear worship leader role in the Bible, especially in the New Testament. That alone should give us pause. We can glean some important principles from Old Testament Levites such as Asaph, Heman, Jebuthun, and others who led in song at the tabernacle and temple (1 Chronicles 16:1–7, 37–42; 25:1–8). But we can't transfer everything they did then to what we do now. They foreshadowed the perfect priest, Jesus Christ, who fulfilled everything their ministry pointed to (Hebrews 9:23-28). . . . The Psalms tell us volumes about what corporate worship should say but aren't as clear on how it's led, other than saying it involves instruments. And some people question whether that still applies[28]

This means, as strange as it sounds, having the role of "music leader" filled in the local church is not an absolute necessity. That's right, a church can be vibrant, healthy, biblical, and lack a "worship leader." Notice, I did *not* say a church can be healthy without singing. The expression of worship through song is non-optional for the local church, but that doesn't mean guitar-slinging-*you* are non-optional.

This reality hit home for me recently during one of our church's Sunday morning gatherings. On this particular Sunday we completely scrapped our usual full band; we stripped everything down to one piano and a couple of singers, and we sang classic hymns. Although, if you were there, you may not have even noticed that the piano and singers were on stage, because, as soon as the rest of the congregation began to sing every other sound was swallowed up into the glorious sound of corporate singing (which is something to shoot for in every worship service more on this later). In that moment I was struck by how un*essential* a "worship leader" is in the grand scheme of ecclesiology.

No, this isn't some practical joke in which you're tricked into reading five chapters into a book only to be slapped across the face with, "Got you! Your job has no biblical warrant and you are a joke. Pack up your guitar; you're through!" I don't think that all of this means our role has to be kicked to the curb, but it *does* have two very important implications about how this role is defined.

ELDERS, DEACONS, AND WORSHIP DUDES?

First, it means that we must stop treating the role of a "worship leader" as an office of the church. It's not. There are elders, and there are deacons. Either the musical-worship leader is a pastor, or he is not. This means, dear reader, that if you do not meet the qualifications of an elder and have not been ordained for pastoral ministry, you have no business being called the "worship pastor." So often we treat this role as a halfway-point between the layman and the *real pastor*. So the music leader exercises much more authority and influence than the average church member without ever being held to the standards—or given the responsibilities—of pastors.

Even if you have been involuntarily placed in this odd position of suspended animation, take this charge to heart: be very careful. I would encourage you to either talk to your pastors about ordination and actual pastoral ministry or stubbornly insist on making sure your pastors are *pastoring you* in this area. By this I mean, make sure the major decisions surrounding your ministry (new songs, new band members, major changes to the order of worship, etc.) are being cleared by your pastors. Even if they simply approve what you suggest without any real consideration, the procedure of intentionally submitting yourself (and your ministry) under their pastoral authority is not just a formality; it actually matters.

Why? Because as pastors they are ultimately responsible for the well-being of the congregation and *you are not* (Heb 13:17). Don't get me wrong; if you start introducing songs from the Mormon hymnal and spouting Arianism between songs, you will certainly be held accountable before God for your sinfulness in this area. But your *pastors* will be held responsible for the damage done to the flock of God, which has been entrusted to *them* (not you). And by the way, your own confidence in the soundness of your theology is irrelevant. If the flock hasn't been entrusted to you, then your unchecked decision making as a music leader is like gambling with someone else's loan money. For the safety of your own pastors, and their eternal stewardship, please, be responsible.

And for any pastors who may be reading, if you have left some poor soul in the position of assuming this quasi-pastoral role, charting the waters of song selection and order of worship alone, please repent. Either demote the guy and accept your pastoral responsibility in this area, or promote the guy (assuming he meets the qualifications of eldership) and let him rightfully take on the pastoral responsibilities. Understand that *you* are held accountable to God for the way your people are being taught through song. They are being conditioned on how to pray, how to express adoration, how to think about God, and so many other things through the songs they sing. If they are taught an untruth through the misled ramblings of your worship dude or through unorthodox song lyrics, *that's on you*. Do you feel the weight of that?

Are you allowing an unequipped individual to watch over the flock of God—which God purchased with *his own blood*—of which the Holy Spirit has made *you* an overseer? If you don't take it from me, take it from Mark Dever, who once said to an entire stadium full of pastors: "Pastor, you need to realize that *music is your business*. If you think that music is not your business, you have misunderstood your call to teach your congregation."[29] Take care, brother pastor, to ensure that you are not squandering your stewardship from God. You have a stake in how the congregation worships through song, so act accordingly.

CORPORATE, CORPORATE, CORPORATE!

Second, this means that the "worship leader" is useful insofar (and *only* insofar) as he gives the congregation a vehicle to worship the living God corporately through song. We don't find any trace of a "worship leader" in the New Testament. But we *do* find instructions for the corporate body of believers to sing in the New Testament (Colossians 3:16, Ephesians 5:18-21). So a "worship leader," in order for his role to be justified in any sense, needs to be understood as—and *function as*—merely a facilitator to help the congregation obey the command of Scripture to sing corporately.

This needs to sink in deep. You are not there to be seen, recognized, or adored. A "win" for you is not an impressed "audience." Corporate participation is the central aesthetic aim to what you're doing as a musician. This means that it is way more important for the person in the back to feel a sense of collected connection with the whole gathered body than it is for him to hear the breathy inflection of your voice. This is true even if your congregation doesn't want it to be!

I stress this last point because I have been in situations where most of the congregation would be much happier to listen to a performance than to worship corporately through song. If forced to choose between (a) quietly listening to the jams of a talented musician and (b) raising their voices in unison to create a thunder-clap-like roar of praise, they choose the former. If you find yourself in a situation like this, your responsibility is not to keep them happy. You aren't doing a service to the non-singing congregation by simply singing on their behalf. What we need in our churches are music leaders that are so committed to the corporate nature of worship through song that they would gladly step off the stage (never to return again) if that brought about greater corporate participation.

SERVING WITH SONG SELECTIONS

So let's look at some practical implications here. I said that a musical-worship leader's position is justified only if he serves to facilitate obedience to the commands of Scripture to corporately sing praise to God. So how is this done? With respect to song selection, I offer the following comments.

Pick orthodox, theologically rich songs. To state the obvious, all the corporate participation in the world doesn't mean anything if the content of your songs are theologically poor. A massive group of people roaring out blasphemy are no less blasphemous because they're roaring together. Likewise, sincerity of heart doesn't matter if what people sing is sincerely wrong.

So it's absolutely necessary that you pick songs that aren't lying about God and his work. However, it's not enough to simply say this. Al Mohler once observed, "Many churches are looking for songs that include no heresy. That's not enough. We need songs that have genuine content." Mohler then added, "Some of the songs I've heard *have no capacity for heresy*."[30] I struggle to find a better statement to capture the quintessence of modern worship songs: they don't even have the capacity for heresy. May it never be said of the songs you lead your congregation in. If the lyrics of a song in question are able to fit onto a post-it note, and are more likely to elicit head-scratching than wonder and worship when read aloud, the song probably needs to be abandoned. Shoot rather for songs that are true and rich, the content of which is not simply tantalizing when the mood is right.

Leave your people stuffed with rich, meaty, fatty theology; leave them belching orthodoxy. In doing so, you are giving your congregation the twofold gift of offering them a legitimate vehicle by which they can worship God (they are singing true things about God to God—ascribing worth to him duly) and of teaching them about God. In other words, you and your congregation will have the opportunity to externalize sound theology while at the same time internalizing sound theology.

Cover a broad spectrum of topics. It's not enough to just play a couple of theologically rich songs that only cover a couple of topics. Scripture is chock-full of theology, and our worship songs should give proper expression of this fact.

- Sing songs about the glory of God, the power of God, the holiness of God, the justice of God, and the wrath of God.
- Sing songs about the love of God, the grace of God, the mercy of God, the kindness of God, and the provision of God.
- Sing songs about God's trinitarian nature; songs about the Father, Son, and Spirit—songs that center on God's oneness *and* threeness.

- Sing songs about Jesus.
- Sing about the incarnation in which God, without ceasing to be God, became man.
- Sing about Christ's active obedience and the righteousness therein earned and imputed to us.
- Sing about Christ's passive obedience and the wrath of God propitiated.
- Sing about the bloody cross and the empty tomb.
- Sing songs in anticipation of his second coming.
- Revel in grace.
- Revel in the gospel.
- Revel in the church the gospel creates.
- Sing songs about suffering and perseverance.
- Sing songs about death and heaven and eternity.

All this means you're going to have to play the long game here. You can't have a set list with all brand-new songs every week; you'll need to slowly work toward giving your people a robust reservoir full of soul-nourishing songs, so enjoy the process!

Cover a broad spectrum of emotion. Let the Psalms be your guide. Sing songs of outright, unflinching, enthusiastic praise and adoration. Sing songs of thanksgiving—songs that recount God's perpetual kindness and mercy. Sing songs that capture dumbfounded awe and wonder. But also sing songs of deep heartache. Sing songs that capture the feeling of crawling through mud and broken glass to drag your lamentations to the feet of God. Sing songs that express desperation for deliverance and songs that express the kind of deep remorse that only a recognition of the sinfulness of sin can explain.

And let's be honest here, you're going to have a much more difficult time finding these kinds of songs. If the present tenor of modern evangelical worship music is any indication of the state of modern evangelicalism, we have to conclude that modern evangelicals are allergic to the concept of lamenting to God. When inheriting a church's "playlist" as a music leader, one thing you'll never have to worry about is an excess of songs of mourning. Somehow songs that express anything less than euphoric, bubbly, I'm-so-happy-I-just-can't-even happiness have become banished entirely. "You don't have to sing lyrics that are coherent, but they *better not* express sorrow!"

Will you join me, dear reader, in breaking that trend? Don't believe the lie that says songs of lamentation and heart-broken confession and cries of sorrow are irreverent in corporate worship. God doesn't seem to think they are. The same God who inspired his hymnal to include lyrics like, "Make a joyful noise to the Lord, all the earth! Serve the Lord with gladness! Come into his presence with singing!" (Ps 100:1–2) also inspired words like, "Be gracious to me, O Lord, for I am in distress; my eye is wasted from grief; my soul and my body also. For my life is spent with sorrow, and my years with sighing; my strength fails because of my iniquity, and my bones waste away" (Ps 31:9–10).

(*Hiatus: On Lament*)

I'll even take it a step further and say that if you are going to holistically succeed in your role of helping your congregation to worship the living God, you must incorporate songs that cover a broad spectrum of emotion. I've already given one reason for singing corporate songs of lament (namely, that the Psalms—which were inspired by God for the purpose of congregational singing—include lamentations), but let me give you two more.

First, this is how we weep with those who weep. In 1 Corinthians 12 Paul beautifully describes the organic and symbiotic relationship between members of the body of Christ. He essentially debunks the notion that *any* member of the body is expendable. You can't declare independence from any other member of church; when one member is neglected, abandoned, or hurt, the whole body is neglected, abandoned, or hurt. "If one member suffers," Paul says, "all *suffer together*; if one member is honored, all rejoice together." (1 Cor 12:26) The fact is, we have members in our congregations who are suffering. According to Paul's logic, then, *we are all suffering*. This is what it means to "bear one another's burdens." When God supernaturally "knits us together in love," he ties our nerve endings together; we feel the pain of our brothers and sisters. When we hear of a member's child who's been sexually abused, *we* feel the wind get knocked out of us. When another month goes by, and still, a couple in our congregation hasn't conceived, *we* feel our hearts sink into our stomachs with disappointment.

Therefore, if such suffering occasions the lamentation of our individual brothers and sisters, it's entirely appropriate for us to lament corporately. I may not have suffered the loss of a child, but according to Paul, when one member has suffered the loss of a child, we—as a congregation—have experienced a great loss. We are brought into their struggle, so *their* suffering becomes *our* suffering, and *their* lamentation becomes *our* lamentation.

Additionally, our congregations do not exist within a cultural vacuum. We exist in the already/not yet of Christ's kingdom, and the "not yet" is from time to time acutely palpable. We are sojourners whose citizenship belongs to kingdom of Christ, but with our "Green Cards" in hand we roam the kingdom of darkness, and there we see and experience a lot of disturbing events that shake our communities and nation and world. We, as citizens of heaven, are not by virtue of our citizenship immune to the tragedies of this world. As a community of Christians on this earth, we experience the macro injustices common to the rest of the world. *Our* nation champions infanticide. *Our* nation still reels with racial injustice—both past injustices with ongoing ramifications and current injustices. *Our* communities are attacked by shootings and other forms of terrorism. So not only does congregational lamentation give our local churches a language to express the grief of its individual members, it also gives a language to express the grief of the larger earthly communities our congregations exist within.

Second, we need to learn how to grieve well. For better or for worse, our congregational songs teach theology. Our regular corporate songs cause theology to seep into us in a way that cannot be quantified. Since lamentation should be informed and governed by right theology, one of the ways our members will learn how to grieve well is by having it modeled and scripted for them in theologically sound songs of lament.

Obedience to the command to "rejoice in the Lord always" looks different from season to season. Picture the young mom of a newborn baby, holding her child and singing "It Is Well With My Soul." That's her rejoicing "when peace, like a river, attendeth her way." But what about when a young mom, through sobs and tears, sings "It Is Well With My Soul" after she miscarries? That's her rejoicing "when sorrows, like sea billows, roll." And much of the Christian life is simply preparation for suffering. Even if some members don't personally need a language of worshipful lamentation at this very moment, they will eventually. I want my members to be prepared to know what to pray and how to process their grief when they are blindsided with unimaginable tragedy.

Make no mistake, there is a uniquely Christian way to suffer. A Christian's suffering is no less painful by virtue of his Christianity, but there is a difference between a Christian's lamentation and a non-Christian's. We do not grieve as those without hope. When we cry "how long, O Lord?" we have been assured by God himself that the answer—whatever else it may be—is not "forever." A Christian's grief never leads to absolute despair because a Christian's suffering is never meaningless—there is no such thing as an affliction that doesn't prepare for us an "eternal weight of glory beyond all comparison."

If a Christian lamentation is nothing else, it is a longing gaze heavenward—it is a grief and discontentment for the present death and destruction that Adam's sin occasioned, and it is the expectation for what God promised: that our eyes will be wiped of our tears and our broken hearts will be bound up. Christian lamentation is the shameless acknowledgement that things are not as they should be and things are not as they will be. Through the eyes of faith—which are red and puffy and wet and tired with grief—we look forward to a reality that our eyes of flesh insist is a wish dream: "We will feast in the house of Zion! We will sing with our hearts restored. 'He has done great things,' we will say together! We will feast, and weep no more,"[31] "when these trials give way to glory, as we draw our final breath, we will cross that great horizon, clouds behind and life secure. *And the calm will be the better for the storms that we endure.*"[32]

Pick songs in which content and tune fit. This is an aesthetic element, but aesthetics are important. There needs to be a sort of fittedness to the songs we sing. So if you sing a song that has content of outright praise and exaltation and adoration and gratitude, make sure the tune doesn't sound like it belongs in a funeral procession. Likewise, if you want to sing a song of lament, make sure it's not an upbeat *boom-chuck*. It's just plain confusing. Most of the time you only run into this oddity in the case of refurbished hymns. For some strange reason, modern worship bands are notorious for taking glorious, joyful historic hymns and giving them a *slightly* different tune (just different enough to embarrass you when you sing along) and replacing every major chord with a minor one. This is a mistake. There is an intrinsic quality about music in which melody naturally corresponds with emotion, and emotion naturally corresponds with content. If this were not the case, Jesus' analogy would make no sense whatsoever, "We played the flute for you, and you did not dance; we sang a dirge, and you did not mourn." (Matthew 11:17)

Pick songs that are singable. Perhaps you have a favorite song, the lyrics of which minister to your soul deeply. Maybe it's theologically rich, it stirs your affections for Christ, the tune marries perfectly with the content, and perhaps you personally sing it as an expression of worship all the time. The fact is, if the song isn't singable, none of those other elements matter.

Corporate songs are intended to be sung corporately. Now, what constitutes as singable, may vary from context to context. And what constitutes as singable in a congregation may be subject to change as the people mature in their musical range. My point here isn't to define precisely what is or is not singable; rather, I want to point out that there *is* a definition for each and every church.

The most frequent offenders that break this important rule are: (a) songs that are too high and (b) songs that are too complicated. You need to know your people and know what they can handle.

We can tease out this principle with even further implications. It may mean that you need to refrain from extemporaneous vocal runs if your people aren't used to it. This isn't always the case, of course; I have worshiped at churches that are more "soulful" than others, and in those gatherings the singers on the stage may break from the predictable melody to do a vocal run and it doesn't faze the rest of the congregation one bit (because they are just as likely to break from the predictable melody to do a vocal run). But, in general, it's best stick to the boring old melody; often a break can distract and interrupt the congregation.

If, for some reason, it's hard for you to sacrifice your favorite groovy run or your favorite super-complicated song, or if it's hard for you to drop your favorite song to G because you like the way it sounds when you sing it in B or A, consider the possibility that idolatry is the real problem. It doesn't matter if you sound better or impressive or skillful. By the way, the point of whether or not the congregation likes it is irrelevant; the question is, does it help or does it hinder corporate participation? Excellence, in and of itself, is not a virtue in the business of leading corporate worship through song. *Undistracting* excellence is what you're after.

SERVING WITH THE ENVIRONMENT

Having set out some pastoral suggestions on song selections, I now turn our attention to some of the broader aesthetic elements of environment. Don't make the mistake of thinking this is unimportant. Aesthetics matter. Environment matters. Obedience to the biblical commands of corporate worship may be helped or hindered by these elements. Even the evangellyfishy silliness I have lampooned all throughout this book demonstrates an understanding of the importance of environment. The intentional manipulation of these aesthetic elements to create an environment of isolated, absent-minded fuzziness is a hindrance to theologically rich, edifying, corporate worship through song. But the answer to this problem is not to disregard these circumstantial elements altogether; rather, the answer is to bring all of these elements under the lordship of Jesus. To this end, I offer the following few suggestions.

Leave the lights on. Why? Let me answer that question with a question: why turn the lights off? The answer to that question ranges from mere preference to principled answers that I would argue misunderstand the meaning and purpose of corporate worship. People may prefer for the lights to be left off because they feel more comfortable with singing if they know that others can't see them. This is the reason hairbrushes have the ability to transform into microphones in the hands of undercover pop stars behind locked bathroom doors, but as soon those doors open, the magic wears off in an instant. But there is a *massive* difference between singing into a hairbrush alone and singing with the corporate body of Christ.

If you find yourself being asked to turn the lights off because such and such member is embarrassed to sing in front of others, gently assure said member that *nobody cares* about what he or she looks or sounds like. People shouldn't be critiquing how other people look while singing in the gathered assembly anyway; that's not what we assemble for. The fear of being seen and the desire to be seen both stem from the same prideful misunderstanding of the corporate gathering; namely, that the individual is the center of attention. Both the desire to disappear into darkness and the desire to be showcased by a spotlight should not be welcomed in the corporate gathering, because the corporate gathering isn't about the desires of *any one member.*

Churches also turn the lights off because they are intentionally trying to foster an environment where individual Christians can isolate themselves from one another. What they're after is private, secret, isolated encounters with Jesus. This is not a wrong desire in and of itself, but it's not what the corporate gathering is for. We don't corporately gather together with the intention of ignoring one another. We come together to worship *together*. Think about corporate worship in terms of an open warehouse rather than a labyrinth of cubicles.

It may further be argued that turning the lights off still may contribute to a corporate feel because dimming the sense of sight may increase the sense of sound. That is, if we turn the lights off, you may get the sensation that you are surrounded by a sea of people singing. That's good, right? Not exactly, because what we're after is not a corporate gathering of worship with a nameless faceless mass of people. You're worshiping with brothers and sisters that you should know and love and share burdens with. *Member* is not a superfluous term that refers to a stranger who happens to spend a couple hours in the same room as you every week.

Earlier in the book I described how corporate worship through song teaches and admonishes, and I referred to the scenario of a mother of a cancer-stricken daughter, worshiping God for his sovereign goodness. I made the point that you have to *know* the people you worship with in order to be edified by their worship: how can I be uniquely edified by such parents when I see them worship if I don't know that their daughter is battling cancer? But the other side of the coin is this: how can I be edified by said mother in corporate worship if I cannot see her praising God for his sovereign goodness? In the end, I turning off the lights in the worship service hinders the corporate nature of the gathering.

Less is more. Be simple, music leader. Again, we want to strive for undistracting excellence because our role is simply to give the corporate body a vehicle by which it can worship God. Distractions happen in different ways. To make a technical mistake (e.g., singing the wrong line, playing the wrong note, starting with the wrong rhythm, etc.) is one way that your playing may be a distraction. However, playing an extremely complicated, elaborate version of a song (fully loaded with face-melting guitar shreds and drum solos) may also be distracting. "It sounds cooler" is not a good enough reason to pick the most complicated arrangement of a particular song. There's wisdom in simplifying songs to fit the size of your band, the skill of your band, and the size of your congregation.

Also, practically, you really should avoid anything that unnecessarily distracts *you* and your team. To lead worship is to worship in front of the church. So just like the rest of the congregation, if you are distracted by other elements (making sure you don't mess up on a technically difficult arrangement, for example), you cannot meditate on the lyrics of the song. If you are helped to see and savor Christ by simplifying the arrangement, you will be serving your congregation by doing so. Simplicity is your friend, so welcome it with open arms.

Serve with the levels. I am not well versed in the world of sound tech. It's actually kind of embarrassing how little I know about running the soundboard, considering how long I've been leading worship through song, but it is what it is. You may be like me in this regard, but even if you don't know all the technical aspects of the sound system, the levels in the worship service are your business. You need to be in open communication with the AV team (if there is one) because they play a massive role in what you do. As such, you need to be on the same page for what constitutes as a "win" and what doesn't in the musical portion of the service. Just because something sounds better in the service doesn't make it the right move.

Let me give you a very simple example: the band should not be so loud that the congregation can't hear itself sing. It doesn't matter if the band sounds good. The band shouldn't play well so that it can sound good, the band should play well to facilitate corporate involvement. Someone might push back on this and argue that a significantly loud band helps corporate involvement because people feel more comfortable with singing if they are confident that other people won't hear them. But again, this isn't actual corporate involvement. Instead, it is merely creating a false sense of isolation, which is *not* what we want. It's handing everyone a hairbrush, locking them in the bathroom, and telling them to sing their little hearts out in private. That's not the point of corporate worship.

It's far less important for the person in the back of the room to hear *my voice* than it is for him to hear *our voices*. It is not really crucial for every person in the room to hear the ambient tone of the electric guitar, but it is absolutely imperative that every person in the room get a sense of collective vocal unity. All this to say, running sound for a concert and running sound for a corporate worship service should be very different. This principle should be extended from the area of volume to reverb and delay and everything else.

CONCLUSION

Obviously, much more can be said about all of these things. I've not tried to be exhaustive in this chapter; rather, my intention was to give you some principles to better understand your role as a music leader. What you understand your role to be (consciously or subconsciously) will determine what decisions are made for the corporate gathering and how they are made. If you understand yourself to be a servant who facilitates congregational obedience to God's instructions for corporate worship, the rest follows.

CHAPTER 7

DISSECTING THE SERVICE

In a recent sermon I heard on Leviticus, I was reminded afresh why we worship the way that we do at my church. In this sermon the pastor summarized the story of Nadab and Abihu in chapter 10—the story of Aaron's two sons who tried to worship God in an unauthorized way and were immediately struck dead for their presumptuous thinking. How arrogant it was for them to think that they were entitled to innovate ways of approaching God distinct from the meticulous prescription God had graciously given. "I told you how I intend to be worshiped," God was saying in the dramatic act of "roasting" these two fellows, "if you truly desired to express your love and adoration for me in worship, you would have simply obeyed my commands." This story portrays stark picture of the holiness of God—we dare not approach him flippantly or by any means other than those which he has provided.

What, you may be asking, does this have to do with how we conduct our worship gatherings at my church? I'm not saying that our church—or any church—should be worried about fire falling from heaven if our worship service doesn't accord with Leviticus. In fact, the most relevant application of this story for twenty-first century Christians has little to do with how we conduct our corporate gatherings, but rather with the exclusivity of Christ. This story tells us that God provides the means for communing with him, and a healthy fear of his holiness ought to compel us to stick to those means. In Leviticus 10 the means were the preceding (and proceeding) instructions for animal blood sacrifices and ritualistic cleansings. Today, the means is the blood sacrifice of Jesus Christ (Heb 10:19-25). The primary application, therefore, is this: don't you dare try to commune with God by virtue of anything but the blood of Jesus. If you try to predicate your intimacy with this God on anything but the blood of the Lamb (e.g., your works, your sincerity, your piety, etc.), you are committing the same sin as Nadab and Abihu.

This is why we ought to exhort one another often to come to Christ with empty hands; to self-justify your hearing before God with your own works is not only foolish (you could never do enough to justify a hearing before such a holy God), it's also blasphemous. It's tantamount to saying that what you offer is better than (or improves upon) the blood of Jesus.

However, there is a secondary application from this story, which goes along with the first. At the very least, Leviticus 10 tells us that God cares about how people worship him. This is why I generally identify with what theologians call the "regulative principle" of worship.[33]

This simply means that we want Scripture to regulate not just the *who* of corporate worship, but the *how* of corporate worship. And by "regulate," I don't simply mean, "define what's off limits." Rather, I'm saying that Scripture has told us what Christians are to do when they gather together to worship, and as a principle, I believe we should commit to doing *only* what Scripture commands.

By using the term regulative principle I place myself squarely within the crosshairs of self-appointed web theologians who live to police the church world for accurate categorizations. For many of these folks, bless their souls, I'm immediately disqualified for claiming to subscribe to the regulative principle because I do not believe that Scripture commands that we sing Psalms exclusively. However, for simplicity, I'm not going into the weeds of who should or shouldn't be allowed to identify with the regulative principle; rather, I'm concerned merely with answering the question: Does Scripture tell us how Christians are to worship corporately or does it not? Yes, Scripture *does* instruct the people of God on how they are to worship corporately, even for New Testament Christians who are not covenantally bound to the Mosaic Law.

And what does Scripture command for New Testament believers to do corporately? We are commanded to:

1. read the Scriptures (1 Tim 4:13);
2. teach/preach the Scriptures (1 Tim 4:13; 2 Tim. 4:1–2);
3. pray (1 Tim 2:1; Acts 2:42; 4:23–31);
4. sing (Col 3:12–17); and
5. participate in communion and baptism (1 Cor 11:23–34; Acts 2:38; Matt 28:19)

That's it. That's what we should be doing when we gather together corporately. Our liturgy should not include anything that doesn't fit comfortably inside those five corporate commands. And by "comfortably," I mean that we shouldn't try to squeeze movie clips, dance routines, or that guy who throws paint on a canvas to depict what looks like nothing at all until he flips it right-side-up to reveal he was actually painting a very Caucasian Jesus into the category of "teaching/preaching Scripture." There's not a single quote from *The Office*, for example, that could ever be followed up with "thus sayeth the Lord!"; so a clip of *The Office* would be totally out of step with the purpose of the corporate worship gathering

Now, some churches may venture outside of these five elements that the New Testament explicitly commands for their corporate worship services.[34] They may even do so without shifting from the gospel as their central point of emphasis. Should such churches anticipate facing a similar fate as Nadab and Abihu? I don't think so. In fact, I wouldn't even go so far as to say that they are being explicitly disobedient to Scripture. But I do think they are wrong not to subscribe to the regulative principle for three reasons.

Frist, the church is God's. The regulative principle fosters a corporate understanding that a particular congregation belongs to God, while the alternative fosters a corporate understanding that a particular congregation belongs to the congregation (or, more often, the leadership of the congregation). God purchased the church with his own blood and has subsequently placed her under the stewardship of elders (Acts 20:28). This means that church leaders cannot do with their flocks as they please; they do not own their churches. The regulative principle establishes an impulse among our church leaders to ask, "What would the owner of this church like for us to do?" I do not think the same could be said of the alternative principle, which looks to Scripture for prohibitions but intrinsically makes it possible to leave the door open for churches to operate according to the whims of popular opinion or the fleeting charisma of personalities.

Second, God's church is governed by God's Word. The regulative principle reinforces the conviction that Christians live their lives positively directed by the Word of God rather than merely guarded by the prohibitions of God's Word. The alternative principle, in my estimation, inherently reinforces the natural sinful perspective that Christianity can be defined by what people are not allowed to do and that life is ultimately to be governed according the autonomous wishes of the individual. That is, what makes a Christian a Christian can be reduced to a list of rules that he does not break. Conversely, the regulative principle is an object lesson in and of itself, teaching that Scripture does not merely set boundaries for how Christians should not live but also directs Christians positively for how they should live. It's not merely that our lives are our own and, as long as we don't transgress God's boundaries, we can do what we want. No;

rather, we are slaves of Christ, and he lays rightful claim to every square inch of our lives. The regulative principle reminds us of this fact.

Third, God cares about how we worship. The regulative principle assumes that God actually cares about how he is worshiped. Though our means of approaching God (the shed blood of Jesus) and Nadab and Abihu's means of approaching God (the Levitical priestly offerings) are different, the God we are worshiping is one and the same, and thus the manner in which we worship him should be the same (i.e., with reverence and special attention to what he has said about worship). Further, Leviticus tells us what kind of God he is. He is a gracious God who provides what he requires (a means), and he is a holy God who cares about how he is worshiped.

On the cusp of the new covenant's arrival, Jesus informs the Samaritan woman at the well, "The hour is coming, and now is, when the true worshipers will worship the Father in spirit and in truth, for the Father is seeking such people to worship him" (John 4:23). He does not say that the Father is seeking worshipers who worship him "however they see fit." We have to look to the Word of God to see what Christ means when he says the Father wants worshipers who worship "in truth." Our starting point has to be Scripture. If we begin with self and then merely look to Scripture for approval or disapproval, we do not cast the appropriate shroud of suspicion on the preferences of sinners—even if we are sinners who are saved by grace.

THE ORDER OF WORSHIP: AN EXAMPLE

You may affirm that corporate worship must have (and *only* have) public ***Scripture reading***, ***prayer***, ***singing***, ***preaching*** and ***teaching***, and observances of ***the ordinances***,[35] but at the end of the day, you need to organize those elements into a weekly order of worship, a weekly routine.

This routine is what we mean when we say "liturgy," and every element matters. In reality, even "non-liturgical" Churches have liturgies—more times than not, it's a liturgy that is absent-mindedly adopted. Opening song. Announcements. Greet your "neighbor." Pass the bucket for tithes. Two more songs. Sermon. Response song.

As musical-worship leaders, we don't want to do anything absent mindedly; we want to have an explicitly biblical/gospel-informed reason for everything that we do. Hear me clearly: leading worship is more than picking the right songs; it is also about the arrangement of the service. When the founding pastors of my own church were originally crafting the liturgical structure of our services, long before we began to even gather on a regular basis, they were pushed back to the drawing board on several occasions with one resounding impulse: *we need more gospel in the flow.*

At present, our services stick to the following liturgical format:

- Call to worship
- Song of praise
- Scripture reading
- Songs of response
- Corporate confession
- Private confession
- Assurance of pardon
- Song of thanksgiving
- Sermon
- Communion
- Song of response
- Benediction

Below I've broken down each element of our liturgy to explain why we repeat such an activity week by week and how it is intended to adorn the gospel. I offer you the following liturgical template as an example. You may find yourself in the situation of actually crafting the order of worship on Sunday mornings, or you may find yourself in the situation where you have inherited an order of worship you have no control over. In either case, I hope this exploration will help you to both appreciate what your church is already doing and to consider possible options for your future ministry.

Call to worship. This is what begins our service. Of course, we often arrive before the call to worship to enjoy the company of one another, but the formal service doesn't start until the call to worship. Why do we start this way? Because, as I explained in chapter 2, worship is essentially comprised of two elements: revelation and response. Worship is the act of responding to that which has been revealed. So if we truly gather together with the intention of worshiping our Triune God, we need see him first! This is why our call to worship is always a Scripture reading. God has revealed himself through his Word, and if we intend to see him—so that we can respond appropriately—we must look there.

The call to worship is also an act of mutual upbuilding. We are calling ourselves, and each other, to fix our eyes on God to see how glorious he is! It's us saying to one another, "God is glorious and worthy of praise! Look at him! Isn't he glorious and worthy of praise?! Yes! He *is* glorious and worthy of praise, so let's praise him for his glory!" This is why the person leading in the call to worship will begin the call as an address to the congregation, and then the congregation will join the call as an address to both the congregation and to God. We are starting with God and unifying our voices around him in such a way that we are corporately affirming that he is worthy to be the center of our attention.

So in the call to worship we are simultaneously declaring to God that we consider him worthy of the praise we are about to ascribe to him, and we are asking for him to "incline [our hearts] to [his] testimonies, and not to selfish gain!" (Ps 119:36) The call to worship is intrinsically a de-centering act; we are communicating from the outset that our gathering is about ascribing worth to God, not merely pleasing ourselves.

Song of Praise. After a call to worship, how could we not respond with a song of praise? This song typically focuses on the bigness of God. We praise him for one of his divine attributes—his holiness, his power to create the cosmos or redeem his people, his unfathomable love, etc. He is a massive, unimaginably glorious God we have just been called to worship, so we gladly do just that.

Focusing on the bigness of God necessarily brings gravity into the service. I'm tempted to go on a tangent here about reverence, but I'll simply say this: you should *rage against* "glibness" in your services. We should have zero tolerance for vanity and frivolity in our songs. Joy? Yes. Exuberance? Absolutely. Cheesiness, presumption, or triviality? God forbid it! Why? Because we are worshiping *God*. If our songs aren't marked by a palpable gravity, we may not be worshiping the God of the Bible. *This God* is a holy, consuming fire, the sight of whom often causes people to fall facedown in terror and dread. He has told us that acceptable worship in his sight is marked by "reverence and awe," (Heb 12:28–29) so we dare not offer him anything less.

Scripture Reading. Again, Scripture is supposed to be a central element for the gathered church, so we want to engage it often. Why read an extended passage here, after the first song and before the second? Simply this: we want for Scripture to actually, functionally direct our service. It would be easy to read a passage of Scripture at the beginning, take credit for having a "biblically based" service, and then run off and do whatever we please with the remainder of our time. But that's not what we want. Rather, we want to sandwich our Scripture-filled songs with Scripture readings, Scriptural preaching and Scriptural obeying. In other words, we read right here in the service to indicate that Scripture isn't merely the foundation of our service; rather, it comprises the content of our service.

Song(s) of Response. Again, after we've read about this glorious God and what he has done, we are compelled to express his worth through song, so we'll typically sing two more songs here. These songs may be songs of praise, thanksgiving, lamentation, or meditations on the gospel. In any case, we want for all of our services to be marked by at least a few bloody songs that adorn Jesus, and this is often a great place to embody such a commitment.

Corporate Confession. Confession is another kind of prayer and thus fits "comfortably" in the category of prayer for what I have described above as the regulative principle. At my church we participate in corporate confession for three reasons:

First, after reading about, and singing about, the glorious, holy, Triune God and all that he has accomplished in the gospel, we are compelled to confess our sins. The gospel works itself out in our lives, and as we meditate on what God has done in Christ—to interrupt our sin and rebellion and helplessness, to die the death we should have died, and to bring us into his Father's family as brothers and sisters—it brings about ongoing repentance. There is a contrast between who God is and who we are, and with the clearest view of that contrast—with a full awareness of the fact that we often persist in faithlessness despite God's unshakable faithfulness—we repent. However, this kind of repentance isn't a shame-filled, guilt-ridden kind that leaves groveling criminals trembling for fear of what the judge's verdict might be, but rather a hopeful and genuinely sorrowful kind of repentance that leaves a child humbly heartbroken over disobeying his dad.

Second, the whole of a Christian's life is marked by continued repentance. At our church we want our corporate gatherings to be a microcosm of the Christian life. Confessing and repenting corporately is a way for us to set a precedence and an expectation for what we do as a church. We are teaching one another what kind of people we are—namely, a confessing people; a people who bear their sins to one another and to God; a people who do not hide their sin but rather search for it, bring it out into clear daylight, and execute it in public; a people who never despise weakness and neediness on the one hand, and who never minimize the sinfulness of sin on the other. In confessing corporately, not only are we praying corporately, we are teaching each other what to do with sin—that is, we shameless bring it to Jesus, the only one who can actually deal with it.

And third, when we corporately confess our sins to God, with one mind and heart, we are owning the fact that we are not the hero of the story. Don't miss the counterintuitive irony about the situation: after three songs of singing with hands in the air, bellowing with loud triumphant-sounding voices, we decide to corporately admit our failures and our neediness and confess our sins to God. Our community is an oxymoron. It is an army of soldiers who fight by dying. We proudly come together to sing about how weak and desperate we are. With boldness and shameless enthusiasm, we are united by our utter allegiance to—and dependence upon—a King who conquers death by being conquered by death. This is the folly of the cross—and the power of God unto salvation—and it is helpful to be reminded of this week after week. Corporate confession is thus a joint exercise in humility.

Private Confession. After we confess our sins corporately, we allow for such an act to set in and do a work on us at the individual level. This extended period of private, silent meditation is intended to be a period of unearthing. Week after week we come together as a people who have been battered and bruised by sin (be it sins we see, sins committed against us, or sins we commit ourselves), and this period of the service is an opportunity—within the context of corporate worship—to do business with God. I fully expect that through the course of the preceding liturgical elements (call to worship, Scripture reading, corporate songs, corporate confession), God has been at work convicting his people and revealing idols. Because of this, it is important that we have the opportunity to respond to such conviction and revelation. So in private confession, we do just that.

Assurance of Pardon. In this part of the service the leader reads a passage of Scripture that addresses God's forgiveness of sinners in Christ, followed by a very brief explanation and declaration of God's grace. The assurance of pardon is even more important than the confession itself, for it is the outright promise that those in Christ have a rock-solid justification. Despite the subjective reality of what we may be feeling when we confess our sins, the assurance of pardon reminds us that an *objective* reality has been holding us secure throughout (even before confessing): if we are in Christ, we are forgiven.

In this way, the person who is leading the liturgy is speaking as an ambassador of Christ to administer priestly comfort and peace. And it is not presumptuous to do this either, for the entire declaration is predicated not on the speaker but on Christ and his atoning work. So the assurance of pardon fits both under the command to read the Scripture and also the command to teach/preach the Scripture; the speaker not only reads the text, he goes on to apply its various implications to the believers present ("*your* sins are forgiven through Christ!").

One other interesting aspect of our assurance of pardon is that it is offered suddenly, without any warning, while our members are still privately confessing. Recently, I had a member ask me why we do things this way. "When you starting reading Scripture, I'm not really sure what the procedure is," he said, "like, are we still praying or not?" The abruptness of the assurance of pardon at our church is intentional. Why does the leader not say "amen" before administering the assurance of pardon? Simply this:

we want our members to be interrupted by grace. We want the very first thing they hear, almost in a disruptive sort of way, to be God's gracious words of assurance for those who have been united to Christ by faith.

This is, in and of itself, an opportunity for us to demonstrate the gospel once more: God did not wait for us to clean ourselves up and make ourselves presentable before taking it upon himself to redeem us; rather, he came while we were still weak and enemies. Likewise, I have no intention of waiting to administer the assurance of pardon until after the congregation has divulged all of its sins to God. I want the congregation to hear the grace of God drowning out their sins like a bear-horn while their confessions are still on their lips. This why the assurance of pardon will often include something like, "those sins *that you have just confessed*, are already forgiven in Christ. They have been nailed to the cross and buried in the grave, and you are one with the resurrected Christ!"[36]

Song of Thanksgiving. Does anything make more sense than a song of thanksgiving at this point? I mean, honestly, when we've just been interrupted with such grace—when we've had such a declaration of God's mercy showered upon us as a people, unexpectedly and scandalously—singing a song of thanksgiving is the most logical thing we could do. So this song is typically one of the most explicitly gospel-rich songs we sing.

Sermon. Since the bulk of our time gathered is actually spent here (and since this is not a book about preaching, but corporate worship through song), I don't think it's necessary to elaborate extensively on the purpose and centrality of the preaching event. I do think it's important, however, to point out that the sermon is not just an act of the preacher; it is an active demonstration of worship from the congregation as well. We are not merely passively listening while the pastor worships in front of us; we are actively submitting ourselves to the Word preached, and as such we are worshiping.

In this event the pastor is reading, preaching, and teaching the Scriptures, and in that act he is standing as an ambassador of God, stewarding his message for his church. This means that to the degree the pastor faithfully exposits the text, and to the degree that he faithfully communicates God's will and God's heart with his explanations, exhortations, and emphases, God speaks through him. As such, a tremendous amount of humility and reverence is required by the pastor (can you imagine a weightier responsibility than heralding God's Word? There isn't one!), but also by the congregation.

Communion. Communion is one of the clearest acts of obedience a Christian can participate in (1 Cor 11:23–26, Matt 26:26–28), and it is one of two central visible signs a Christian can observe as an identifier of his Christianity (baptism being the other). Communion is also a potent reenactment of the gospel; every broken piece of bread testifies to the broken body of Jesus, every drop from the cup testifies to the shed blood of Jesus, and every person who consumes the bread and drink is a testimony to the saving work that Jesus accomplished at the cross.

So the essential elements of communion visually demonstrate the gospel, but also the corporate act of communion depicts what the gospel *does*—namely, it creates the church. Every time we take communion as an entire body, we are uniting ourselves around the broken body and shed blood of Jesus. Such a unifying act proclaims what God has done in Christ; it declares, "*This* is what Christ's body was broken for, *this* what Christ's costly blood purchased: *a church*."

Try to keep this in mind, by the way, the next time you take communion. Often we're tempted to make communion an ultra-personal time of introspection, but it's a command that can only be carried out by *a corporate body*. So rather than going introspective, look up and take note at what communion represents: each of the people who tear and eat and drink are trophies of God's grace—each having his or her own distinct story—and they all collectively make a masterfully crafted mosaic. Often you will find individuals who may have nothing in common to speak of, save Jesus Christ, taking communion side by side, thereby testifying to divine engineering. *Only God could build the church*, and when we take communion we testify of this.

Lastly, when we take communion as a body we look not only back to the past—at what Christ has done on the cross—and we look not only at the present—at the church God is building—we also look forward to heaven. This world, as it now stands, is not our home. Remember what we explored in chapter 4: we are looking forward to our eternal homeland. Yet every local church is like a heavenly embassy; gathering together on Sunday morning rightly feels a little bit like coming home. However, such a gathering is necessarily marked with a hint of longing. We long for the day when our communion with one another isn't merely a weekly visit on a heavenly embassy that exists in an alien country. Presently, we gather weekly, but in that day we will worship in the presence of God forever. Presently, we offer prayers and thanksgiving and intercession, and all of our rejoicing is co-opted with sorrow, but in that day King Jesus will wipe away every tear. Presently, we eat (sometimes stale) bread and drink (sometimes cheap) wine (or store-bought grape juice), but in that day we will celebrate the massive, cosmic, wedding feast of the Lamb! Communion aids us in this worshipful longing, in which we simultaneously enjoy God for what he has done and look longingly for what God has promised to do.

Song of Response. The song of response is, again, a logical step. Remember, worship is revelation and response. At this point of the service, we have just finished basking in the revelation of several Scripture readings, Scripture-filled songs, an exposition and proclamation of Scripture, and the visual proclamation of Scripture's central message (the gospel, as seen in the act of communion). In other words, at this point we are stuffed from gorging ourselves on revelation. Response is demanded by our souls! So, in this last song, we gladly oblige that impulse.

Benediction. In the last element of the benediction, we conclude our services with an act that at the least constitutes the command to pray and teach (and often, if the benediction is directly from Scripture, we also fulfill the command for public Scripture reading). The benediction is both a challenge to obey the Word preached and a petition for God's blessing in that endeavor. In the benediction we ask for the grace of God to pursue godliness in the coming week.

The above is just one example of what an intentional order of worship might look like; by no means should you take this example as dogmatic instruction. The point is that your order of worship simply needs to be intentional. You communicate what you value as a musical-worship leader and as a church not only by the songs you sing and the sermons you preach but also by the way you structure your services.

GOSPEL SATURATION

There is another thing that needs to be said about the general ethos of the service: a healthy service is a gospel-saturated service. Remember, the central message of the entire Bible is the gospel. Thus, if we truly subscribe to the regulative principle (the principle that insists on only including that which Scripture commands for corporate worship), we will not only orbit our services around the essential elements of corporate worship—prayer, singing, reading Scripture, teaching/preaching Scripture, and the ordinances—if we *truly* subscribe the regulative principle, we will do all of these things with a distinct emphasis on Scripture's central theme: the gospel—such an emphasis is biblical fidelity.

What might this look like? It may simply look like arranging your services in such a way that your liturgy is itself a retelling of the gospel. You may have even noticed that the liturgy above loosely mirrors the gospel itself:

- *Creation*: In the beginning, God = *Call to worship*
- *Fall*: Enter sin and its devastating effects = *Confession*
- *Redemption*: Christ comes, nailing sin to the cross and burying it in the grave! = *Assurance of pardon*
- *Restoration*: Christ is making all things new = *Song of thanksgiving*
- *Consummation*: We eagerly await the return of our Lord = *Communion*

In all of this, we want every person who participates in our liturgy to walk away deeply impressed, not by the oratory skills of the preacher, or the band, or the sweet facilities, but by Jesus. This is why, at our church, we frequently say, "We want you to leave this place more in love with Jesus than when you walked in." Those comments are not cheap platitudes. They refer to the point of our whole gathering: we come as a body to hold fast to the Head, "from whom the whole body, nourished and knit together through its joints and ligaments, grows with a growth that is from God." (Col 2:19)

TRINITARIAN WORSHIP

I would be remiss if I concluded this chapter without saying a word on the importance of making the corporate worship gathering explicitly trinitarian. Why should our worship be explicitly trinitarian? Because

God is Triune. If we do not worship a Triune God, we do not worship God. There are several important things modern evangelicalism is pretty weak on at present, and a robust and full-throated love for the Trinity is certainly one of them. You want proof? Well, *The Shack* has been an astronomical success among evangelicals.

I rest my case.

But seriously, what's the big deal? The Trinity is deeply mysterious. Isn't it an *advanced* topic? No. At least, the Trinity *shouldn't* be viewed as a strictly *advanced* topic. The reason being, God is fundamentally triune, so if we want to grasp any aspect of theology (the study of God), we must do so within the context of trinitarian categories.

Let me give you an example. As Christians, we should be *all* about Jesus. We should long to point each other to Christ and we should long to see unbelievers place their faith in Christ. But just who is this Jesus that we are pointing one another to and inviting people to put their faith in? He is Jesus, the *Son of God*. He is irreducibly *God the Son*, which means he's got a Father—the eternal Father. And not only that, but also this Jesus lives and communes with his Father through the eternal Spirit, and when we put our faith in this Jesus, we get his Spirit as our seal.

In other words, you can't simply "save the Trinity for later." To point to Jesus is fundamentally to point to the second member of the Trinity. "When you start with the Jesus of the Bible, it is a triune God that you get. The Trinity, then, is not the product of abstract speculation: when you proclaim Jesus, the Spirit-anointed Son of the Father, you proclaim the triune God."[37] When you search for Jesus, what you find is the Trinity.

Furthermore, we should be all about the Trinity in our worship not only because God is triune—and thus to worship God is to worship the Trinity—but also because the gospel—the central message of the Bible that ought to permeate our services—is the good news of what the *Trinity* has done!

The history of redemption is brimming with unique trinitarian activity: The *Father*—not the Son, nor the Spirit—elects a people for his Son and sends his Son to redeem and reconcile them to himself (Eph 1:3–5; Rom 8:29; 2 Tim 1:9). The *Son*—not the Father, nor the Spirit—submits to the Father, is incarnated, lives a perfect life, makes atonement for his elect, and ascends to the right hand of the Father to receive all authority in heaven and on earth, and subsequently sends the Spirit as a seal on his people (John 6:38; 8:28–29; 15:9–10; Heb 7:23–26; Acts 2:32). The *Spirit*—not the Father, nor the Son—submits to the Son and regenerates and illumines and seals the church (John 14:16–17; 16:7–15; Eph 1:13; Titus 3:5).

If you go back and review all of the verses referenced (and you should), you'll see that every part of the gospel involves all three persons of the Trinity, occupying their own distinct role. You don't get the gospel when you try to make sense of it with generic theism, and you don't get the gospel when you try to make sense of it with autonomously acting gods; the gospel is accomplished by none other than the eternal Three-in-One.

Additionally, even the benefits of the gospel are trinitarian! Michael Reeves is helpful here:

> For it is not just that we are brought before the Father in the Son; we receive the Spirit with which he was anointed. Jesus said in John 16:14 that the Spirit "will bring glory to me by taking from what is mine and making it known to you." The Spirit takes what is the Son's and makes it ours. . . . And so, as the Son brings me before the Father, with their Spirit in me I can boldly cry, "Abba," for their fellowship I now freely share: The Most High *my* Father, the Son my great brother, and the Spirit no longer Jesus' Comfort alone, by mine.[38]

So what does all of this mean for the corporate worship gathering? It means that the God we worship must be explicitly identified as the Triune God of the Bible. For my own part as a music leader, I do everything I can to assure that our worship services are shaped by the Trinity. I want our public prayers to be shaped by the Trinity (we ordinarily pray in this formula: to God the Father, through the atoning and intercessory work of God the Son, by the power of God the Spirit). I want our confessions and assurances of pardon to be shaped by the Trinity. I want our calls to worship and benedictions to be shaped by the Trinity. In short, I want my church to *know* (and *love*) that the God I invite them to worship with me on Sunday morning is *triune*. Every element of the worship service (from the songs we sing to the prayers we pray) conditions the congregation for how to think about God. Therefore, we must labor to ensure that such conditioning has a consciously trinitarian shape.

CHAPTER 8
BATTLING FORGETFULNESS

We are forgetful creatures. We spend most of our time from rut to rut, apathetic toward the magic around us and in us. We exist in a universe spoken into existence out of nothing. Trinitarian beauty is woven into every part creation, and every existing fact testifies to God's existence and his goodness. Our response?

Yawn

For unbelievers, this indifference is understandable. Their default disposition, after all, is to suppress the truth about God (Rom 1:18–23)—they cannot help it, it is in their DNA to whistle in the dark; no one needs to teach them how to resist the overwhelming revelation in which they are immersed. And of course there, but for the grace of God, go we. Yet, we could say, there, *despite* the grace of God, go we still. Because, despite having had our eyes opened by grace to recognize God's activity in the world, we respond to his artistry with slow blinks.

But it's not just the magic of general revelation that we ignore. As Christians we can absentmindedly read the *words of God* in the special revelation of Scripture.

God's words.

Words, that *God* has *spoken* and *written.* We can read a book authored by God absentmindedly (go ahead and read that out loud if its ridiculousness didn't strike you the first time). For Christians, these words contain promises of assurance. Promises that belong to us in Christ; they're our (new) birthrights! Promises like:

> Who shall separate us from the love of Christ? Shall tribulation, or distress, or persecution, or famine, or nakedness, or danger, or sword? As it is written, "'For your sake we are being killed all the day long; we are regarded as sheep to be slaughtered.'" No, in all these things we are more than conquerors through him who loved us. For I am sure that neither death nor life, nor angels nor rulers, nor things present nor things to come, nor powers, nor height nor depth, nor anything else in all creation, will be able to separate us from the love of God in Christ Jesus our Lord. (Rom 8:35–39)

It's a funny thing that words like this can become familiar to our ears. Maybe funny isn't the right word. Odd, or perplexing, perhaps? Better yet, tragic. Yes, let's go with tragic. It is tragic that we can read these words, or hear them read, and remain unphased and indifferent. When I stop to think about my own attitude toward these claims in Scripture, I'm embarrassed. How jarring does God have to be to shake me out of my lethargy?

God: Hell itself cannot separate you from my love, Sam.

Me: *Yawn*

We need to be reminded, not just of what the gospel is, but what it *means*. We need to regularly be grabbed by the shoulders, shaken, and screamed at: ARE YOU PAYING ATTENTION?!

Good preaching does this. Good preaching hijacks our imagination and subverts our default mental barriers to present the familiar gospel to us in less familiar ways. Have you ever found yourself finishing a preacher's gospel presentation once it starts? Ever heard your inner voice reciting his words before he does? This is a sure sign that you have been given the gospel message in a truncated fashion time and time again, and the result is that you check out. You stop paying attention.

Of course, this isn't entirely the preacher's fault; he's preaching the gospel, and that should be enough! We should be tender to it. The reality of our indifference is an indictment. But it rests on an axiom that we have little control over: when you repeat the same word over and over again, it stops sounding like an intelligible word. And when the gospel is repeatedly presented in the same truncated fashion, it soon begins to resemble a lecture from Charlie Brown's teacher.

On the flip side, have you ever found yourself beginning to finish the preacher's gospel presentation only to be jolted into awareness of the sermon because of a slight tweak in the language? A little provocative swerve? You think he's going left in an illustration but instead he goes right? When a preacher does this, he is casting light on the same familiar gospel from an unfamiliar direction, thereby exposing you to shades and contours you had either forgotten about or had never noticed before. The gospel never changes, but like a diamond that refracts light in a thousand ways, we get to be freshly mesmerized by this never-changing gospel when it's presented to us from different angles.

This, by the way, is why the gospel needs to be spoken into our lives by one another. Everyone holds the gospel a little differently, and every time the timely word from a brother or sister in Christ reminds us of the grace of God afforded us by the life, death, and resurrection of Jesus, we get to see this same, perfect diamond from a different perspective. One brother reminds you of *this* implication. Another sister reminds you of *that* implication. The end result is that you get a far richer flavor of the gospel than you would have if you were all by your lonesome. So for this last chapter, I'm going to hold up the gospel for you and slightly tilt it in the light so as to highlight some of its loveliest sides.

THE GOSPEL FOR MUSIC LEADERS

The gospel that you sing and read and pray and display as a music leader is the same gospel you need as an image-bearer. There is no separate standard for justification that you are expected to meet which your members are not. I will have failed in my ultimate aim to serve Jesus's church if you, dear reader, put this book down feeling the crushing weight and pressure of everything "you need to do." Your greatest need is not a game plan. Your greatest need is the gospel.

So, friends, let us fix our attention squarely on the riches of the gospel. If you are a believer, what you find here in this chapter is true for you. Full stop. You could completely make a blunder every single instruction I've given up until this point, and still, 100 percent of the realities in this chapter are yours to revel in. They can't be touched by your performance as a music leader. Before you try to apply any of the principles laid out in this book, it is most important that you spend a little bit of time soaking in the benefits afforded to you in gospel. Here are four benefits to consider:

First, in the gospel, you have been totally remade by God through regeneration. Notice the first three words in 2 Corinthians 5:16: "from now on." There is a time indication given which shows us that something fundamentally is different. Back then we regarded people "according to the flesh," but from now on we regard no one according to the flesh. Back then we regarded Christ "according to the flesh," but from now on we regard him thus no longer.

What causes this change of perspective? What happened to Paul to enact the change, where he *once* regarded Christ according to the flesh but *now* regards him thus no longer? Regeneration. "Therefore, if anyone is in Christ, he is a new creation. The old has passed away; behold, the new has come." (2 Cor 5:17; see also John 3:1–15; Titus 3:5)

As you grow up, your opinions on many issues change and develop and deepen. You come to new information and you respond to it accordingly. Most of your life is marked by steady, incremental growth. *This is not what happens in regeneration.* In regeneration, God *creates*. In regeneration, God makes something new. Have you ever wondered what it must have looked like from the vantage point of the angelic hosts to see God speak the universe into existence with a breath? What it was like to see stars flung *out of* nothing like gigantic paint splatters on a canvas of pitch black?

Well guess what? That same *ex nihilo*—out-of-nothing—creative power is present in every single conversion. This is why Paul speaks about conversion like this: "For God, who said, 'Let light shine out of darkness,' has shone in our hearts to give the light of the knowledge of the glory of God in the face of Jesus Christ" (2 Cor 4:6). Paul is quoting from Genesis 1, where we read about how God spoke the universe into existence. And he explicitly says that same God who spoke light into the darkness of the infinite void at creation speaks light into the darkness of the dead heart for every new creation.

This means, Christian, God has created something new in you; it is a spiritual life, a faculty that recognizes God's activity. You were born of flesh, now you are born of water and Spirit. You were dead, now you are alive. You were a goat, now you are a sheep, cared for by the Good Shepherd. You were chaff, awaiting to be burned, now you are wheat. You were an inhabitant of the domain of darkness, now you are a citizen of Jesus's kingdom. In the gospel you don't receive a makeover, you receive a new birth; you aren't simply remodeled, you were a broken-down home that he completely demolished and rebuilt from scratch—only now you are far more glorious than before. You truly are not the same person you were before Jesus got to you. Do see the shimmer of regeneration?

Second, in the gospel, you are united to Christ. The doctrine of union with Christ is the most underappreciated doctrine of salvation for most Christians. This beautiful doctrine teaches that somehow, mysteriously and supernaturally, Christians have been united to Christ in his life, death, and resurrection (Eph 1:3–14; Rom 6:5–6; Gal 2:20; Col 3:1–4). When Christ died, you—along with all your sin and also with all your *sinfulness* (i.e., your efforts to justify yourself with your own actions or words, your self-righteous arrogance, your lust, your pride, etc.)—died as well. When Christ was nailed to the cross, you—with all your sin and sinfulness—were nailed to the cross. When Christ was buried in the grave, you—with all your sin and sinfulness—were buried in the grave. And when Christ was resurrected, you—with<u>out</u> your sin and sinfulness—were resurrected with Christ.

Paul uses baptism to illustrate this doctrine of union in Romans 6:1--1:

> What shall we say then? Are we to continue in sin that grace may abound? By no means! How can we who died to sin still live in it? Do you not know that all of us who have been baptized into Christ Jesus were baptized into his death? We were buried therefore with him by baptism into death, in order that, just as Christ was raised from the dead by the glory of the Father, we too might walk in newness of life. For if we have been united with him in a death like his, we shall certainly be united with him in a resurrection like his. We know that our old self was crucified with him in order that the body of sin might be brought to nothing, so that we would no longer be enslaved to sin. For one who has died has been set free from sin. Now if we have died with Christ, we believe that we will also live with him. We know that Christ, being raised from the dead, will never die again; death no longer has dominion over him. For the death he died he died to sin, once for all, but the life he lives he lives to God. So you also must consider yourselves dead to sin and alive to God in Christ Jesus."

Paul emphasizes, specifically, that when we were united with Christ, he took our old selves and buried them in the grave and left them there to rot as worm food. Subsequently, Christ brought us up as new men and women who are now free to walk in obedience to Jesus. "You have died to sin," he is saying, "though sin used to be your slave master, it no longer has dominion or authority over you because the body that was bound to its chains is now six feet under." A slave master can't bark orders at a corpse. As far as sin is concerned, you're a dead man out of whom it cannot force labor. That's what union with Christ earns—freedom from the compulsory power of sin: it doesn't mean that you won't sin or won't *want* to sin, but it does mean you don't *have* to sin. We no longer have that pitiful excuse, "I couldn't help it." In our union with him, Christ took that excuse and he turned it into fertilizer.

By the way, we should be careful not to abstract this doctrine and its benefits from the person of Jesus. It's the real Jesus to whom you are united: the perfect God-man, who lived a sinless life and died on a Roman cross, who was buried in a Mediterranean grave, who was resurrected three days later, and who is now seated at the right hand of God the Father, where he intercedes for you. *That's* the Christ to whom you were united.

This beautiful doctrine means that on account of your union with *this* Christ, you are separated from your sin by a vast chasm. Between you and your sin lies some two thousand years of human history, miles of earth and sea, some thirty years of perfect God-man living, death, resurrection, and an eternity of God's gushing love and favor and kindness toward you. *All of this* lies between you and your sin. And your sin can never traverse that chasm to mark you because it can never come to Christ, and you are in him. Your portion is his portion. Your inheritance is his inheritance. You could no sooner be rejected by God the Father than Jesus could be, because you are cloaked in Jesus. You could not sooner be enslaved to sin than Jesus could be, because Jesus murdered your old sin-owned-slave-body in his own death and resurrected you as a free person. Do you see the brilliance of union with Christ?

Third, in the gospel you have been reconciled to God. Just what does this union with Christ—this status as a new creation—mean for our relationship with a righteous God? Everything, that's what. As Christ hangs on the cross on your behalf, Christian, a legal verdict takes place which fundamentally changes your position before God. "For our sake," says Paul, "he made him to be sin who knew no sin, so that in him we might become the righteousness of God" (2 Cor 5:21). Objectively, judiciously, and legally, the sentence God renders on your behalf is: righteous. Justified. This is what justification means; no more guilt, no more debt, no more crime on the books that elicits wrath to loom over your head because those debts and records of offenses have been nailed to the cross in Jesus Christ (Col 2:14). And this new justified status wins you nothing less than reconciliation with the God you previously had every reason to dread and cower away from.

Never forget, Christian, that God was under absolutely no obligation whatsoever to do any of this reconciling work on your behalf. We have to get this: we will never understand just how precious the gospel is until we understand that reconciliation didn't have to happen. The scandal of the gospel is that reconciliation didn't have to happen, but, "for our sake," *did.*

In the name of reconciliation, God sent Christ not only to bear the wrath that our sin earned but also to earn a righteousness for us to bear. This is how reconciliation happens for you, Christian: God reconciles himself to you in Christ. God writes himself into the story to reconcile himself back to his rebellious characters. God steps down from his glorious throne as Almighty Creator and reconciles himself to his own lowly creatures. God takes off his robes of righteousness and so that he might drape them over us.

And the initiative is completely one-sided, which is the way it has to happen (e.g., verse 18: "All this [being made a new creation] is *from God*, who through Christ reconciled us to himself . . ."). In Romans 5 Paul illustrates the contrast of *our* disposition and *God's* disposition when reconciliation happens (Rom 5:1–11): while *we* are enemies—while *we* are breathing out hatred and venom towards God—*he* laid his life down for us in love. While *we*—clumps of clay; piles of dirt-made-flesh—were violently shouting to God "we *don't want you*," God condescended saying, "I want you." We are recipients of his initiative. You have been reconciled to God because of no other reason than that he has reconciled himself to you.

He is the hound of heaven, who ran you down and overcame your resistance.

He is the conqueror, who defeated you, a wicked rebel, by uniting himself to you, killing you in himself, and resurrecting you in himself as a friend.

You were not a seeker; you were a fugitive, and he, the divine Seeker, hunted you down and restored you to full citizenship of his kingdom.

Do you see the shine of reconciliation?

Fourth, in the gospel you have received adoption. This, to me, is the sweetest reality afforded to us in the gospel. "See what kind of love the Father has given to us, that we should be called children of God; and so we are" (1 John 3:1a). I have spent years reading these words, drawing encouragement and nourishment from them. But it was only after I held my oldest son in my arms for the first time that these words wrapped me up, like a warm blanket of divine love, in a way I had never previously experienced. As I held my son in my arms for the first time, these words knocked the wind out of me. "See what kind of love the Father has given to us, that we should be called the children of God; and so we are." *That's how I am loved? As one of his children?* It seems like this theological concept had been waiting in my soul like a bomb; and it went off right there, with my son in my arms.

The doctrine of adoption is union with Christ with meat on its bones. Union with Christ means that you are *God's child*. You are an heir to God's promises and blessings (Gal 3:23–29). In Christ, your inheritance is as secured as his. This is the very definition of generosity. It is kindness that knows no bounds for Christ to bring us into his divine family, such that we receive the love due him as the only deserving Son. In Christ, we are God's kids.

And notice the trinitarian shape of our worship in Gal 4:6: "And because you are sons, *God* has sent the *Spirit* of his *Son* into our hearts, crying, 'Abba! Father!'" Do you understand what Paul is saying? We are being brought into God's triune love; his love for himself! Because we have the Spirit of God, who makes us children of God, we get to say the same thing as the Son of God: "Abba! Father!" His script is now our script. God the Father overflows with love for Christ, and your adoption means that you are now a recipient of that love. You are united to Christ, who stands under the waterfall of his Father's love for him; since you too are now a child of God, staying dry is impossible.

When Paul says you are "Abraham's offspring, heirs according to the promise" (Gal 3:29), he's saying that the inheritance of communion with God and everlasting life—which are *Christ's* entitled possessions as Son (Gal 3:16)—*belong to you*. They have your name on them, and they are waiting for you. Think about Christmas morning as a little kid: you wake up early in the morning, and there above the mantle are stockings, and one of them has your name on it. And under the tree, the presents wrapped have your name on them. Why? Because you are a child of your parents. You are an heir. No one else can touch those blessings, because they are yours, given to you by your father and mother.

Oh! What amazing grace it is to be brought into the family of God! To have blessings with your name on them *in his house*! Just bask in the reality that *you are a child—an heir, an inheritor—of God Almighty*. And here's the thing: what makes your station so dang sweet is that you weren't entitled to *any* of it. You are now, rightfully, a legal and familial recipient of his love, and you got here—in this family, in this home—not by being born into it, but by being *adopted*. You were a nameless orphan, who laid claim to absolutely nothing, and *just like that*, God swooped you up into his arms, gave you a key to his house, invited you to rummage through his refrigerator, and bestowed on you his name.

You don't have to tip-toe past his office and hope you don't disturb him. You don't have to worry that your requested audience with him will be met with, "I'm too busy." He's not stuck with you; it was his idea to include you into his family, and he sent the eternal Son to shed divine blood on your behalf with all of your imperfections and sins and idiosyncrasies in mind. He knew exactly what he would have to work with in bringing you into his family, and he happily chose to go through with it; he signed the adoption papers with a grin. It is his delight to raise you in his family, and like any good father, he intends to shape you into holiness within the context of warm, paternal love.

To be a Christian is to be adopted into the family of God. It means to be one of his kids. And he will never abandon his children. So be encouraged, Christian! Be encouraged that your station as a child of God isn't contingent on your ability to obey; it's contingent on his willingness to love you—and *He has loved you*. So walk in uprightness from there; as a child of God, knowing that your heavenly Father looks at you—in a similar way that I look at my son—and says, "That one's mine."

Do you see the brilliance of adoption?

CONCLUSION

Labor to never lose sight of these precious realities, music leader. You need the same gospel your people need, and the great news is that God delights to meet our need. If we bring him our emptiness, he'll fill it to the brim with himself. In the gospel our needs are met. We needed righteousness, and Jesus's life met that need. We needed atonement from sin and freedom from the law, and Jesus's death on the cross met that need. We needed newness of life and adoption into God's family, and Jesus's resurrection met that need. Our God delights to meet our needs.

Furthermore, our God is trustworthy. This is not a wishy-washy God we worship. He has made a promise to you in Christ, and he is more trustworthy than your insecurities. He is more trustworthy than your failures. He is more trustworthy than your worst and best days. He always keeps his promises, and he has bound himself to you in Christ with the most solemn of promises—he has staked his reputation on your salvation. You can rest your head on that promise tonight and sleep soundly. You can collapse onto that promise and let it bear your full weight when you are tired and exhausted and storm tossed.

He loves you.

CONCLUSION

A CALL TO ARMS

It is no small thing to lead God's people in worship through song. What we engage in is not the warm-up act. Worship is the telos of *all* Christian activity. The intended end of preaching is worship. The intended end of discipleship is worship. The intended end of evangelism and missions and biblical-theological study is worship. It's what we exist for, not only as Christians, but as human beings.

It is true that corporate worship through song is merely one of the ways we fulfill this grand purpose of ours, but it is nevertheless a central one. The gift that you give the people of God—if you serve faithfully and biblically—is truly incalculable; you afford them the opportunity to live out their sole purpose as human beings by giving them a vehicle by which they can worship God. Or—if you fail to serve faithfully and biblically—you hinder them from living out their sole purpose as human beings by distracting them from worshiping God, thereby robbing God of his due praise. The stakes are that high. We are playing with live ammo, friends, and we must be responsible.

Therefore, given the gravity of what we do, allow me to sound the alarms for faithful service in this area. Take this as a call to arms: all who wield guitars and voices and pianos, all who stand in front of God's people as pointers of glory, all who call themselves music leaders, gird up your theological loins and pursue faithfulness with unrelenting ferocity!

I offer you the following resolutions. Join me, music leader, and may we help to change the landscape of evangelical corporate worship for the glory of God and the edification of his Church.

Resolved, to love the Lord our God with everything we've got.

Resolved, to never tire of the gospel.

Resolved, to pursue biblical literacy.

Resolved, to fight for humility.

Resolved, to put to death the desire to be seen and adored.

Resolved, to use any platform God has graciously given to simply point others back to his glory rather than to vainly showcase our skills.

Resolved, to live exemplary lives in which we regularly fix our eyes on the glories of God and respond to such a vision with adoration and praise.

Resolved, to live in the tension of being broken and built with faithfulness.

Resolved, to settle for nothing less than serious, theologically sound songs for the people that God has allowed for us to serve.

Resolved, to be congregational in our song selection and to prioritize the corporate edification of the church over our personal musical preferences.

Resolved, to make much of the one, triune God and his gospel in every conceivable element of the corporate worship service.

Resolved, to love the Bride of Christ.

Amen.

APPENDIX A

EMMAUS CHURCH: MUSIC TEAM COVENANT

Key Passages:

Psalm 33, 127, 150
John 4:23–24
Isaiah 6:1–7
Ephesians 5:15–21
Colossians 3:16–17
1 Peter 4:10–11

Affirmations and Denials

We affirm that worship is the act of responding to an object with adoration; to ascribe worth to that which is perceived as valuable. We believe that God alone is absolutely glorious—that he is that which is supremely valuable, so we respond to him (who he is and what he has done in creation and the gospel) with worship.

We deny that worship is a solely emotional experience where the end goal is for music to stir us up into an emotional frenzy. We deny, in other words, that true worship equates with singing and that true worship is defined solely by a heightened sense of emotion.

We affirm to lead in worship is to point to the awesome worth of God so that those who see him can respond appropriately.

We deny that to lead worship is to perform Christian songs well.

We affirm that we must live a life characterized by worship. We cannot invite people to see and savor God if we are not first seeing and savoring him ourselves; as lead worshipers, we are inviting the congregation to join us in doing what we are already doing: looking at God's worth and responding in worship.

We deny that we can live inconsistently and worship idols throughout the week and lead others to worship the living God on Sundays.

We affirm that leading worship is more difficult than eliciting emotion by manipulating surroundings, because it requires more of us (our whole lives) and it allows less of us (we can't cause people to actually see the worth of God by means of program or show). Thus, we are "puritans" of sorts; because we believe that our task can only be accomplished supernaturally, and not manipulated by human means, we only want to include that which is governed by the divinely inspired Word of God in our services (we subscribe to the regulative principle at Emmaus).

We deny that the end goal of our worship services can be achieved through means of gimmicks and tricks and the manipulation of circumstances.

We affirm that our worship gatherings are for the corporate upbuilding of the church. Therefore, everything we do, from the volume of our instruments, to the key of our songs, to the lights in the building, to the lyrics that we sing, ought to be governed by a corporate mentality.

We deny that our worship gatherings are intended for individuals to isolate themselves into their own private cubicles with Jesus.

We affirm that this means, questions like, "How good does this sound?"—as important as they are—are less important than questions like, "Does this contribute to corporate participation?" In other words, it's more important for the members of Emmaus to truly feel like they are participating in the act of worship as a necessary contributor than it is for them to be impressed with the band. We (the band) are not performing for them (the rest of the congregation), but rather, we (the entire congregation—band included) are corporately presenting an offering of worship to God.

We deny that the worship gathering is a concert and that it is ever okay for the band to drown out the corporate participation of the rest of the body by bringing attention to ourselves in any way.

Covenant

- I will commit to live an exemplary life free from hypocrisy.
- I will commit to live a life of worship, so that the Sunday morning worship service will serve as the natural overflow of a God honoring week.
- I will commit to pray fervently for Emmaus that God would be glorified in her members, activities, and worship gatherings.
- I will commit to regular intake of Scripture, so that the Word of Christ will dwell in me richly.
- I will commit to please God rather than man through my musical worship ministry.
- I will commit to using the platform of a musician to serve the congregation with my gifts and passions rather than to perform in front of them.
- I will commit to relentlessly make war on the sin of pride, the need to be seen.

- I will commit to un-distracting excellence.
- I will commit to come to practice well-prepared.
- I will commit to making sure my area of responsibility reflects a corporate mentality.

APPENDIX B

SAMPLE ORDER OF WORSHIP

*Read by musical-worship leader

**Read by congregation

Set List for March 12 2017

Call to Worship

*The heavens declare the glory of God, and the sky above proclaims his handiwork. Day to day pours out speech, and night to night reveals knowledge. There is no speech, nor are there words, whose voice is not heard. Their voice goes out through all the earth, and their words to the end of the world. In them he has set a tent for the sun, which comes out like a bridegroom leaving his chamber, and, like a strong man, runs its course with joy. **Its rising is from the end of the heavens, and its circuit to the end of them, and there is nothing hidden from its heat. – Psalm 19:1–6

"All Creatures of Our God and King"

*But you are a chosen race, a royal priesthood, a holy nation, a people for his own possession, that you may proclaim the excellencies of him who called you out of darkness into his marvelous light. Once you were not a people, but now you are God's people; once you had not received mercy, but now you have received mercy. – 1 Peter 2:12

"My One Comfort"
"The Wonderful Grace of Jesus"

Corporate Confession (10–25)

*Have mercy on me, O God, according to your steadfast love; according to your abundant mercy blot out my transgressions. **Wash me thoroughly from my iniquity, and cleanse me from my sin! - Psalm 51:1–2

Private Confession

Assurance of Pardon

*The former priests were many in number, because they were prevented by death from continuing in office, but he holds his priesthood permanently, because he continues forever. Consequently, he is able to save to the uttermost those who draw near to God through him, since he always lives to make intercession for them. – Hebrews 7:23–25

"Now Why This Fear"

Sermon

Communion

"Before the Throne of God above"

Benediction

*Now may our glorious, Triune God bless you and keep you; the Lord make his face to shine upon you and be gracious to you; the Lord lift up his countenance upon you and give you peace.

APPENDIX C

SAMPLE CORPORATE CONFESSION

*Read by musical-worship leader

**Read by entire congregation

Corporate Confession

**Have mercy on me, O God, according to your steadfast love; according to your abundant mercy blot out my transgressions. **Wash me thoroughly from my iniquity, and cleanse me from my sin! – Psalm 51:1–2*

*Triune God, you are very good and very holy. We come to you this morning humbled because we are fully aware of our sins and our insufficiencies. Father, we confess that often we are presumptuous when we come into your presence, thinking that our audience with you something we're entitled to. Remind us that the privilege of prayer is one purchased for us in blood, in order for us to come boldly and soberly. Lord, we confess that we come to you in prayer with hands full of our deeds, thinking that we are sufficient to work our way into your approval. Forgive us for this arrogance; convince us that we can come only to receive grace. Father, we confess also that we often harbor idols. We confess that we often care more deeply how we are perceived by others than how we are perceived by you. Rather than bringing our sins out into the open to be decisively dealt with by you, we hide them in order to maintain our righteous facade for others. Forgive us for thinking that the praise of others is sweeter than sin-forgiving grace. Jesus, we confess also the sins of this nation; we are a people who have sought to heal our sin-seared consciences by pretending that our sin is not sin. Lord Jesus, as your church, we confess that we dishonor you in our hypocrisy; we hide the sins that we shame the world for boasting in. Forgive us for this, Lord Jesus. Teach us to show the world that the forgiveness of sins is infinitely better than the denial of them. May we show the world what it looks like to truly rest in the work that you, Jesus, have done our behalf. Holy Spirit, guide us in this even now, as we confess our own individual sins to you.

Assurance of Pardon

**The former priests were many in number, because they were prevented by death from continuing in office, but he holds his priesthood permanently, because he continues forever. Consequently, he is able to save to the uttermost those who draw near to God through him, since he always lives to make intercession for them. – Hebrews 7:23–25*

*Christian, this morning you have done with your sins the only thing you possibly could do with them: you have brought them to the Lord Jesus. Not only did Jesus atone for your sins on the cross, but with scars on his hands, feet, and side he still lives to make intercession to you. Your works did not save you, and they cannot now condemn you; it is only the work of Jesus that secures your station before the Father. Therefore, if you have been united to the Lord Jesus Christ by faith, it is my privilege, as your brother in Christ, to declare to you that your sins are forgiven.

ENDNOTES

1. Jesus Culture, "Freedom Reigns," *Come Away* (Jesus Culture Music, 2010).
2. Bob Kauflin, *Worship Matters: Leading Others to Encounter the Greatness of God* (Wheaton: Crossway, 2008), 93.
3. N. D. Wilson, *Notes from the Tilt-a-Whirl: Wide-Eyed Wonder in God's Spoken World* (Nashville: Thomas Nelson, 2009), 43. Though N. D. Wilson didn't say this first, that honor goes to the reformer, Martin Luther: "He does not speak grammatical words; He speaks true and existent realities. Accordingly, that which among us has the sound of a word is a reality with God. Thus sun, moon, heaven, earth, Peter, Paul, I, you, etc.—we are all words of God, in fact only one single syllable or letter by comparison with the entire creation. We, too, speak, but only according to the rules of language; that is, we assign names to objects which have already been created. But the divine rule of language is different, namely; when He says: 'Sun, shine,' the sun is there at once and shines. Thus the words of God are realities, not bare words." Martin Luther, *Luther's Works*, vol. 1 *Lectures on Genesis: Chapters* 1–5 (Saint Louis: Concordia Publishing House, 1999), 21–22. Cited by Carl R. Trueman, *Fools Rush In Where Monkeys Fear to Tread: Taking Aim at Everyone* (Philipsburg: P & R Publishing, 2012), 210.
4. C.S. Lewis, *The Problem of Pain* (New York: HarperCollins, 1996), 46.

5. C.S. Lewis, *Mere Christianity* (New York: HarperCollins, 1996), 64.
6. John MacArthur, *Worship: The Ultimate Priority* (Chicago: Moody, 2012), 39.
7. This language of "seeing and savoring Jesus" comes, unabashedly, from the ministry of John Piper.
8. Wilson, *Notes from the Tilt-a-Whirl*, 4
9. C.S. Lewis, *The Great Divorce* (New York: HarperCollins, 1976), 83–84.
10. Joe Rigney, *The Things of Earth: Treasuring God by Enjoying His Gifts* (Wheaton: Crossway, 2015), 63.
11. Charles Spurgeon, *The Treasury of David, Volume 1* (Peabody: Hendrickson, 1990), 274.
12. I take this phrase the title of Vern Poythress's book, *Reading the Word of God In the Presence of God* (Wheaton: Crossway, 2016). This is a fantastic book on hermeneutics that I highly commend.
13. Sebastian Traeger and Greg Gilbert, *The Gospel at Work: How Working for King Jesus Gives Purpose and Meaning to Our Jobs* (Grand Rapids: Zondervan, 2013), 60–61.
14. Rigney, *The Things of Earth*, 138–39.
15. I say "legitimate" because there are obviously some vocations that are inherently sinful. For example, a director of pornographic films, a pimp, or an employee working for a company that fundamentally brings about injustice (such as Planned Parenthood) cannot legitimately work to the glory of God in those vocations because they have, by definition, set themselves up in rebellion to God.
16. I'm borrowing this imagery from C.S. Lewis's spectacular book, *The Great Divorce*.
17. Ibid., 80.
18. Ibid., 102.
19. In this flow of thought, I'm leaning heavily on Joe Rigney's parallel

section in in *The Things of Earth*, 82–83.

20. Ibid., 92.
21. This would include, as Rigney, *The Things of Earth*, 141, points out, even the gifts in culture. ". . . God-exalting, Scripture-guided, prayerful culture is the appointed consummation of God's very good creation. We gladly receive what God gives and thankfully return it to him, sanctified by his Word and prayer. Just as "delight is incomplete until it is expressed," so creation is incomplete until it is faithfully subdued, cultivated, and sanctified by thankful people."
22. Noah Michelson, "These 21 Words About Sex May Be The Most Important Words Miley Cyrus Has Ever Said" *Huffington Post*, June 11, 2015, http://www.huffingtonpost.com/2015/06/11/miley-cyrus-sex-positivity_n_7559964.html.
23. Ibid.
24. The Center for Medical Progress (www.centerformedicalprogress.org).
25. See Acts 5:33–42; 7:54–60; 12:1–5; 14:19–23; 16:16–24; 21:27–28:31; 2 Cor 1:3–10; 2:12–17; 4:7–18, 10; 11:16–12:10; Phil 1:12–30; 3:8–11; Col 1:24–29 just to name a couple of examples.
26. See chapter 2.
27. D. A. Carson uses a footnote as a soapbox to describe this in *Worship By the Book*, and it is just . . . delightful: "When pressed as to the criteria by which [contemporary musical-worship leaders] pick their music, many of these leaders finally admit that their criteria oscillate between personal preference and keeping the congregation happy—scarcely the most profound criteria in the world. They give little or no thought to covering the great themes of Scripture, or the great events in Scripture, or the range of personal response to God found in the Psalms (as opposed to covering the narrow themes of being upbeat and in the midst of

"worship"), or the nature of biblical locutions (in one chorus the congregation manages to sing "holy" thirty-six times, while three are enough for Isaiah and John of the Apocalypse), or the central historical traditions of the church, or anything else of weight. If such leaders operate on their own with little guidance or training or input from senior pastors, the situation commonly degenerates from the painful to the pitiful." See D. A. Carson, "Worship under the Word," in *Worship By the Book*, ed. D. A. Carson (Grand Rapids: Zondervan, 2002), 47 n38.

28. Bob Kauflin, *Worship Matters*, 52–53.
29. Mark Dever, "Getting Out of Babylon Again: The Reformation We Need Today" panel session at Together for the Gospel, 2012.
30. "Getting Out of Babylon Again: The Reformation We Need Today," panel session at Together for the Gospel, 2012.
31. Sandra McCrackin, "We Will Feast In the House of Zion," *Psalms* (Towhee Records, 2015).
32. Matt Boswell, "Christ the Sure and Steady Anchor" *Messenger Hymns, Vol. 2 – EP* (Doxology & Theology, 2015).
33. The Particular Baptists of the seventeenth century did us a great service in summarizing this principle in the 1689 Second London Baptist Confession of Faith: 22:1: "The light of nature shows that there is a God, who hath lordship and sovereignty over all; is just, good and doth good unto all; and is therefore to be feared, loved, praised, called upon, trusted in and served, with all the heart and all the soul and with all the might. But the acceptable way of worshipping the true God is instituted by Himself, and so limited by His own revealed will, that He may not be worshipped according to the imaginations and devices of men, nor the suggestions of Satan, under any visible representations, or any other way not prescribed in the Holy Scriptures."

34. These churches might properly be described as subscribers to the normative principle, which essentially looks to Scripture for general direction but basically affirms that anything that isn't prohibited by Scripture (sin, for example) is fair game for the worship service.
35. Obviously, baptism can't be observed every week, and of course you may or may not agree with me that communion is best observed every week. The point is simply that this ordinance must be observed by Christians in worship; the frequency is less central to the point.
36. See Appendix C for example.
37. Michael Reeves, *Delighting in the Trinity: An Introduction to the Christian* (Downers Grove: InterVarsity, 2012), 37-38.
38. Ibid., 75

Made in the USA
Lexington, KY
22 February 2019